Managing Editor
Mara Ellen Guckian

Editor in Chief
Karen J. Goldfluss, M.S. Ed.

Creative Director
Sarah M. Fournier

Cover Artist
Diem Pascarella

Imaging
Amanda R. Harter

Publisher
Mary D. Smith, M.S. Ed.

TCR 8069

200 Timed Math Tests
ELEMENTARY & MIDDLE GRADES

- Improves proficiency in core math areas
- Provides timed practice options to help students master speed and accuracy
- Builds confidence through competence as students improve math fluency
- Aligns with national standards

Addition
Subtraction
Multiplication
Mixed Math Facts
Fractions
Decimals
Percents

Teacher Created Resources

Author
Mara Ellen Guckian

Teacher Created Resources
12621 Western Avenue
Garden Grove, CA 92841
www.teachercreated.com

ISBN: 978-1-4206-8069-0

© 2017 Teacher Created Resources
Made in U.S.A.

Teacher Created Resources

Table of Contents

Introduction 3
Timed Math Tests Record Sheets 4
Basic Mathematical Properties 7
Addition Table 8
Addition Table (Blank) 9
Multiplication Table 10
Multiplication Table (Blank) 11

Unit 1: Addition
Sums to 10
Tests 1–4 (20 problems each) 12–15
Tests 5–8 (30 problems each) 16–19
Sums from 11 to 18
Tests 9–12 (20 problems each) 20–23
Tests 13–16 (30 problems each) 24–27
Sums from 11 to 20
Tests 17–18 (20 problems each) 28–29
Tests 19–20 (30 problems each) 30–31
Addition Review
Tests 21–24 (20 problems each) 32–35
Tests 25–28 (30 problems each) 36–39
Tests 29–32 (40 problems each) 40–43
Tests 33–36 (50 problems each) 44–47

Unit 2: Subtraction
10 and Less
Tests 1–4 (20 problems each) 48–51
Tests 5–8 (30 problems each) 52–55
Subtraction from 11 to 19
Tests 9–12 (20 problems each) 56–59
Tests 13–16 (30 problems each) 60–63
Subtraction Review
Tests 17–20 (20 problems each) 64–67
Tests 21–25 (30 problems each) 68–72
Tests 26–30 (40 problems each) 73–77
Tests 31–36 (50 problems each) 78–83

Unit 3: Multiplication
Facts for 0 through 2
Test 1 (20 problems) 84
Facts for 0 through 3
Test 2 (20 problems) 85
Tests 3–4 (30 problems each) 86–87
Facts for 0 through 4
Test 5 (20 problems) 88
Test 6 (30 problems) 89
Facts for 0 through 5
Test 7 (20 problems) 90
Test 8 (30 problems) 91
Facts for 6 and 7
Test 9 (20 problems) 92
Facts for 6 through 8
Tests 10–11 (20 problems each) 93–94
Facts for 7 through 9
Tests 12–13 (20 problems each) 95–96
Facts for 10 through 12
Tests 14–16 (20 problems each) 97–99

Review for 0 through 9
Tests 17–20 (20 problems each) 100–103
Tests 21–25 (30 problems each) 104–108
Tests 26–30 (40 problems each) 109–113
Tests 31–36 (50 problems each) . . . 114–119

Unit 4: Division
Facts for Divisors 1 through 5
Tests 1–4 (20 problems each) 120–123
Tests 5–8 (30 problems each) 124–127
Facts for Divisors 6 through 9
Tests 9–12 (20 problems each) 128–131
Tests 13–16 (30 problems each) 132–135
Facts for Divisors 1 through 9
Tests 17–20 (20 problems each) 136–139
Tests 21–25 (30 problems each) 140–144
Tests 26–29 (40 problems each) 145–148
Tests 30–33 (50 problems each) 149–152
Facts for Divisors 10 through 12
Tests 34–36 (20 problems each) . . . 153–155

Unit 5: Mixed Math Facts
Tests 1–5 (20 problems each) 156–160
Tests 6–10 (30 problems each) 161–165
Tests 11–15 (40 problems each) 166–170
Tests 16–18 (50 problems each) 171–173
Tests 19–20 (60 problems each) 174–175

Unit 6: Fractions
One or Less
Tests 1–2 (20 problems each) 176–177
Tests 3–4 (30 problems each) 178–179
Tests 5–6 (40 problems each) 180–181
Greater than One
Tests 7–8 (20 problems each) 182–183
Tests 9–10 (30 problems each) 184–185
Tests 11–12 (40 problems each) 186–187
Mixed Practice
Tests 13–14 (20 problems each) 188–189
Tests 15–16 (30 problems each) 190–191
Tests 17–18 (40 problems each) 192–193

Unit 7: Fraction, Decimal, and Percent Equivalents
Fraction Equivalents
Tests 1–2 (20 problems each) 194–195
Tests 3–4 (30 problems each) 196–197
Tests 5–6 (40 problems each) 198–199
Decimal Equivalents
Tests 1–2 (20 problems each) 200–201
Tests 3–4 (30 problems each) 202–203
Tests 5–6 (40 problems each) 204–205
Percent Equivalents
Tests 1–2 (20 problems each) 206–207
Tests 3–4 (30 problems each) 208–209
Tests 5–6 (40 problems each) 210–211

Answer Key 212–224

Introduction

Learning math facts is not always fun, but it is necessary. To become fluent—that is to commit basic math facts to memory—takes practice. The seven units in this book provide practice pages to help students increase their ability to remember math facts for all operations quickly and confidently.

These practice pages, or tests, can be timed to encourage students to develop fluency. For many, timing can add to the stress of learning. If this is the case for your math learner, don't focus on the time in the beginning. Work on accuracy and don't forget neatness—being able to read test answers is also quite important! If doing a row or a column at a time is all that the student can do at first, that is fine. As confidence builds, so will accuracy and speed. Then you can introduce timing.

For other students, timing the tests seem to be more motivating. Here, the challenge of "winning" is the incentive needed to learn the math facts. Many students are already comfortable using timers on phones and other devices, others will need a little practice in the beginning.

The key to timed testing is setting reasonable expectations. Here are a few options:

- Time the first row a student does and use that time as a guideline for him or her. Continue to time a row at a time until the student is comfortable with the testing process. Adjust either the time or the number of rows as the student progresses.

- Multiply the time it took to do the first row on the page by the number of rows on the page. When setting the time, try rounding up or down to make it more official. Example: round 12 seconds to 10 seconds or 20 seconds per row × the number of rows. You will need to adjust this time when using pages where the number of problems increases.

- Time the class or small group for the first row or page. Estimate the average time it took and use it as a goal. That time will be the time to beat for future tests. Each student can use a recording sheet to keep track of his or her personal times.

- Set a time and have students see how many problems they can complete correctly in that time span. Work to improve the number of correct answers within the given time.

Hopefully, with time, all students will begin challenging themselves to go faster, while remaining accurate and writing clearly.

Recording sheets are provided on pages 4–6 to help student's track their progress. Students can record the time and date, log how many problems they were able to do, and note how many problems they answered correctly on each practice.

Pages 7–11 serve as reference tools for students. A chart is provided reviewing Fact Families and the Commutative, Identity, and Zero Properties on page 7. Copies can be given to students as needed or posted in the classroom or math center. On pages 8–11, Addition and Multiplication Tables are provided for student reference. Blanks are included for students to fill in themselves.

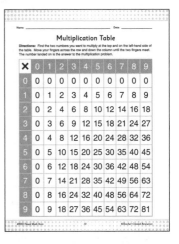

The first four units are Addition, Subtraction, Multiplication and Division. Each of these four units begins with 20-problem practice pages and builds to 30, 40, or 50 problems per page. These beginning units are followed by the Mixed Math Facts review section. The last practice pages in this section have 60 problems per page. The final units focus on Fractions, Decimals, Percents, and their equivalents. Timing for these pages will also need to be adjusted as skills improve.

All 200 test pages are set up in the same manner. Each numbered test page includes the math operation and skill for easy reference. Additionally, the number in the gray circle in the top right corner lists the number of problems on the page. At the bottom of the page, students can fill in the time started and ended, the total time, how many problems were completed, and how many were answered correctly. This information can be transferred to the each student's personal record sheet.

Once students are fluent in the basic facts for addition, subtraction, multiplication, and division, they will be able to master higher mathematical skills more readily and will enjoy—not dread—math!

Timed Math Tests Record Sheet for _____

❶ Addition

Test	Time	Date	#Completed/#Correct
Test 1			____/____
Test 2			____/____
Test 3			____/____
Test 4			____/____
Test 5			____/____
Test 6			____/____
Test 7			____/____
Test 8			____/____
Test 9			____/____
Test 10			____/____
Test 11			____/____
Test 12			____/____

Test	Time	Date	#Completed/#Correct
Test 13			____/____
Test 14			____/____
Test 15			____/____
Test 16			____/____
Test 17			____/____
Test 18			____/____
Test 19			____/____
Test 20			____/____
Test 21			____/____
Test 22			____/____
Test 23			____/____
Test 24			____/____

Test	Time	Date	#Completed/#Correct
Test 25			____/____
Test 26			____/____
Test 27			____/____
Test 28			____/____
Test 29			____/____
Test 30			____/____
Test 31			____/____
Test 32			____/____
Test 33			____/____
Test 34			____/____
Test 35			____/____
Test 36			____/____

❷ Subtraction

Test	Time	Date	#Completed/#Correct
Test 1			____/____
Test 2			____/____
Test 3			____/____
Test 4			____/____
Test 5			____/____
Test 6			____/____
Test 7			____/____
Test 8			____/____
Test 9			____/____
Test 10			____/____
Test 11			____/____
Test 12			____/____

Test	Time	Date	#Completed/#Correct
Test 13			____/____
Test 14			____/____
Test 15			____/____
Test 16			____/____
Test 17			____/____
Test 18			____/____
Test 19			____/____
Test 20			____/____
Test 21			____/____
Test 22			____/____
Test 23			____/____
Test 24			____/____

Test	Time	Date	#Completed/#Correct
Test 25			____/____
Test 26			____/____
Test 27			____/____
Test 28			____/____
Test 29			____/____
Test 30			____/____
Test 31			____/____
Test 32			____/____
Test 33			____/____
Test 34			____/____
Test 35			____/____
Test 36			____/____

Timed Math Tests Record Sheet for _____

3 Multiplication

	Time	Date	#Completed/#Correct		Time	Date	#Completed/#Correct		Time	Date	#Completed/#Correct
Test 1	___	___	___/___	Test 13	___	___	___/___	Test 25	___	___	___/___
Test 2	___	___	___/___	Test 14	___	___	___/___	Test 26	___	___	___/___
Test 3	___	___	___/___	Test 15	___	___	___/___	Test 27	___	___	___/___
Test 4	___	___	___/___	Test 16	___	___	___/___	Test 28	___	___	___/___
Test 5	___	___	___/___	Test 17	___	___	___/___	Test 29	___	___	___/___
Test 6	___	___	___/___	Test 18	___	___	___/___	Test 30	___	___	___/___
Test 7	___	___	___/___	Test 19	___	___	___/___	Test 31	___	___	___/___
Test 8	___	___	___/___	Test 20	___	___	___/___	Test 32	___	___	___/___
Test 9	___	___	___/___	Test 21	___	___	___/___	Test 33	___	___	___/___
Test 10	___	___	___/___	Test 22	___	___	___/___	Test 34	___	___	___/___
Test 11	___	___	___/___	Test 23	___	___	___/___	Test 35	___	___	___/___
Test 12	___	___	___/___	Test 24	___	___	___/___	Test 36	___	___	___/___

4 Division

	Time	Date	#Completed/#Correct		Time	Date	#Completed/#Correct		Time	Date	#Completed/#Correct
Test 1	___	___	___/___	Test 13	___	___	___/___	Test 25	___	___	___/___
Test 2	___	___	___/___	Test 14	___	___	___/___	Test 26	___	___	___/___
Test 3	___	___	___/___	Test 15	___	___	___/___	Test 27	___	___	___/___
Test 4	___	___	___/___	Test 16	___	___	___/___	Test 28	___	___	___/___
Test 5	___	___	___/___	Test 17	___	___	___/___	Test 29	___	___	___/___
Test 6	___	___	___/___	Test 18	___	___	___/___	Test 30	___	___	___/___
Test 7	___	___	___/___	Test 19	___	___	___/___	Test 31	___	___	___/___
Test 8	___	___	___/___	Test 20	___	___	___/___	Test 32	___	___	___/___
Test 9	___	___	___/___	Test 21	___	___	___/___	Test 33	___	___	___/___
Test 10	___	___	___/___	Test 22	___	___	___/___	Test 34	___	___	___/___
Test 11	___	___	___/___	Test 23	___	___	___/___	Test 35	___	___	___/___
Test 12	___	___	___/___	Test 24	___	___	___/___	Test 36	___	___	___/___

Timed Math Tests Record Sheet for _____

5 Mixed Facts

Mixed Facts	Time	Date	#Completed/#Correct		Time	Date	#Completed/#Correct		Time	Date	#Completed/#Correct
Test 1	___	___	___/___	Test 8	___	___	___/___	Test 15	___	___	___/___
Test 2	___	___	___/___	Test 9	___	___	___/___	Test 16	___	___	___/___
Test 3	___	___	___/___	Test 10	___	___	___/___	Test 17	___	___	___/___
Test 4	___	___	___/___	Test 11	___	___	___/___	Test 18	___	___	___/___
Test 5	___	___	___/___	Test 12	___	___	___/___	Test 19	___	___	___/___
Test 6	___	___	___/___	Test 13	___	___	___/___	Test 20	___	___	___/___
Test 7	___	___	___/___	Test 14	___	___	___/___				

6 Fractions

Fractions	Time	Date	#Completed/#Correct		Time	Date	#Completed/#Correct		Time	Date	#Completed/#Correct
Test 1	___	___	___/___	Test 8	___	___	___/___	Test 15	___	___	___/___
Test 2	___	___	___/___	Test 9	___	___	___/___	Test 16	___	___	___/___
Test 3	___	___	___/___	Test 10	___	___	___/___	Test 17	___	___	___/___
Test 4	___	___	___/___	Test 11	___	___	___/___	Test 18	___	___	___/___
Test 5	___	___	___/___	Test 12	___	___	___/___				
Test 6	___	___	___/___	Test 13	___	___	___/___				
Test 7	___	___	___/___	Test 14	___	___	___/___				

7 Fraction Equivalents

Fraction Equivalents	Time	Date	#Completed/#Correct	Fraction Equivalents	Time	Date	#Completed/#Correct	Percent Equivalents	Time	Date	#Completed/#Correct
Test 1	___	___	___/___	Test 1	___	___	___/___	Test 1	___	___	___/___
Test 2	___	___	___/___	Test 2	___	___	___/___	Test 2	___	___	___/___
Test 3	___	___	___/___	Test 3	___	___	___/___	Test 3	___	___	___/___
Test 4	___	___	___/___	Test 4	___	___	___/___	Test 4	___	___	___/___
Test 5	___	___	___/___	Test 5	___	___	___/___	Test 5	___	___	___/___
Test 6	___	___	___/___	Test 6	___	___	___/___	Test 6	___	___	___/___

Basic Mathematical Properties

Understanding basic mathematical properties is necessary to help students develop computational fluency—the ability to "know" the answer to a math fact quickly and without additional computation. The more number "connections" they can make, the greater their ease in memorizing addition, subtraction, multiplication, and division math facts.

Fact Families

Addition and Subtraction Fact Families

$2 + 7 = 9$ $7 + 2 = 9$ $9 - 2 = 7$ $9 - 7 = 2$

Multiplication and Division Fact Families

$2 \times 7 = 14$ $7 \times 2 = 14$ $14 \div 2 = 7$ $14 \div 7 = 2$

Commutative Property

Addition

When adding two numbers, the order of the two addends does not change the answer (sum).

$7 + 2 = 9$ $2 + 7 = 9$

Multiplication

When multiplying two numbers, the order of the two factors does not change the answer (product).

$2 \times 7 = 14$ $7 \times 2 = 14$

Identity Property

Multiplication

Any number that is multiplied by 1 equals that number.

$7 \times 1 = 7$ $70 \times 1 = 70$ $700 \times 1 = 700$

Zero Property

Addition: Zero added to any number does not change the value of the number.

$2 + 0 = 2$

Subtraction: Zero subtracted from any number does not change the value of the number.

$2 - 0 = 2$

Multiplication: Any number multiplied by zero equals zero.

$2 \times 0 = 0$

Division: Zero divided by any number equals zero.

$0 \div 2 = 0$

Name: _____ Date: _____

Addition Table

Directions: Find the two numbers you want to add at the top and on the left-hand side of the table. Move your fingers across the row and down the column until the two fingers meet. The number landed on is the answer to the addition problem.

+	0	1	2	3	4	5	6	7	8	9
0	0	1	2	3	4	5	6	7	8	9
1	1	2	3	4	5	6	7	8	9	10
2	2	3	4	5	6	7	8	9	10	11
3	3	4	5	6	7	8	9	10	11	12
4	4	5	6	7	8	9	10	11	12	13
5	5	6	7	8	9	10	11	12	13	14
6	6	7	8	9	10	11	12	13	14	15
7	7	8	9	10	11	12	13	14	15	16
8	8	9	10	11	12	13	14	15	16	17
9	9	10	11	12	13	14	15	16	17	18

8

Addition Table

Directions: Fill in the Addition Table.

+	0	1	2	3	4	5	6	7	8	9
0										
1										
2										
3										
4										
5										
6										
7										
8										
9										

Name: _____   Date: _____

Multiplication Table

Directions: Find the two numbers you want to multiply at the top and on the left-hand side of the table. Move your fingers across the row and down the column until the two fingers meet. The number landed on is the answer to the multiplication problem.

✗	0	1	2	3	4	5	6	7	8	9
0	0	0	0	0	0	0	0	0	0	0
1	0	1	2	3	4	5	6	7	8	9
2	0	2	4	6	8	10	12	14	16	18
3	0	3	6	9	12	15	18	21	24	27
4	0	4	8	12	16	20	24	28	32	36
5	0	5	10	15	20	25	30	35	40	45
6	0	6	12	18	24	30	36	42	48	54
7	0	7	14	21	28	35	42	49	56	63
8	0	8	16	24	32	40	48	56	64	72
9	0	9	18	27	36	45	54	63	72	81

Multiplication Table

Directions: Fill in the Multiplication Table.

✖	0	1	2	3	4	5	6	7	8	9
0										
1										
2										
3										
4										
5										
6										
7										
8										
9										

Name: _____   Date: _____

4 + 1	3 + 2	4 + 3	5 + 4
1 + 1	2 + 2	3 + 3	4 + 4
5 + 2	3 + 0	2 + 3	1 + 4
5 + 5	6 + 3	7 + 3	8 + 1
2 + 4	6 + 4	7 + 1	8 + 0

Started: Finished: Total Time: Completed: Correct:

Name: _____   Date: _____

5 + 5	8 + 2	2 + 3	3 + 4
10 + 0	3 + 2	4 + 3	6 + 4
4 + 5	3 + 6	2 + 2	1 + 3
5 + 2	6 + 2	6 + 3	9 + 1
2 + 4	9 + 0	7 + 3	6 + 0

Started: Finished: Total Time: Completed: Correct:

Name: _____   Date: _____

$$\begin{array}{r} 6 \\ +\,1 \\ \hline \end{array} \qquad \begin{array}{r} 3 \\ +\,3 \\ \hline \end{array} \qquad \begin{array}{r} 4 \\ +\,4 \\ \hline \end{array} \qquad \begin{array}{r} 1 \\ +\,4 \\ \hline \end{array}$$

$$\begin{array}{r} 1 \\ +\,9 \\ \hline \end{array} \qquad \begin{array}{r} 6 \\ +\,2 \\ \hline \end{array} \qquad \begin{array}{r} 3 \\ +\,7 \\ \hline \end{array} \qquad \begin{array}{r} 0 \\ +\,4 \\ \hline \end{array}$$

$$\begin{array}{r} 4 \\ +\,5 \\ \hline \end{array} \qquad \begin{array}{r} 10 \\ +\,0 \\ \hline \end{array} \qquad \begin{array}{r} 2 \\ +\,3 \\ \hline \end{array} \qquad \begin{array}{r} 8 \\ +\,0 \\ \hline \end{array}$$

$$\begin{array}{r} 0 \\ +\,5 \\ \hline \end{array} \qquad \begin{array}{r} 6 \\ +\,3 \\ \hline \end{array} \qquad \begin{array}{r} 3 \\ +\,0 \\ \hline \end{array} \qquad \begin{array}{r} 6 \\ +\,1 \\ \hline \end{array}$$

$$\begin{array}{r} 5 \\ +\,4 \\ \hline \end{array} \qquad \begin{array}{r} 3 \\ +\,4 \\ \hline \end{array} \qquad \begin{array}{r} 7 \\ +\,1 \\ \hline \end{array} \qquad \begin{array}{r} 8 \\ +\,2 \\ \hline \end{array}$$

Started: _____   Finished: _____   Total Time: _____   Completed: _____   Correct: _____

Name: _____   Date: _____

$$\begin{array}{r} 5 \\ +2 \\ \hline \end{array} \qquad \begin{array}{r} 4 \\ +3 \\ \hline \end{array} \qquad \begin{array}{r} 4 \\ +5 \\ \hline \end{array} \qquad \begin{array}{r} 6 \\ +4 \\ \hline \end{array}$$

$$\begin{array}{r} 2 \\ +2 \\ \hline \end{array} \qquad \begin{array}{r} 3 \\ +2 \\ \hline \end{array} \qquad \begin{array}{r} 3 \\ +7 \\ \hline \end{array} \qquad \begin{array}{r} 5 \\ +5 \\ \hline \end{array}$$

$$\begin{array}{r} 5 \\ +3 \\ \hline \end{array} \qquad \begin{array}{r} 4 \\ +1 \\ \hline \end{array} \qquad \begin{array}{r} 3 \\ +4 \\ \hline \end{array} \qquad \begin{array}{r} 2 \\ +6 \\ \hline \end{array}$$

$$\begin{array}{r} 5 \\ +4 \\ \hline \end{array} \qquad \begin{array}{r} 7 \\ +3 \\ \hline \end{array} \qquad \begin{array}{r} 7 \\ +2 \\ \hline \end{array} \qquad \begin{array}{r} 9 \\ +1 \\ \hline \end{array}$$

$$\begin{array}{r} 3 \\ +5 \\ \hline \end{array} \qquad \begin{array}{r} 6 \\ +0 \\ \hline \end{array} \qquad \begin{array}{r} 2 \\ +8 \\ \hline \end{array} \qquad \begin{array}{r} 1 \\ +8 \\ \hline \end{array}$$

Started: _____ Finished: _____ Total Time: _____ Completed: _____ Correct: _____

Name: _____   Date: _____

3 + 7	4 + 1	3 + 2	4 + 3	5 + 4
0 + 0	1 + 1	2 + 2	3 + 3	4 + 4
0 + 7	5 + 2	4 + 2	3 + 4	2 + 6
4 + 0	7 + 2	3 + 0	2 + 3	1 + 4
5 + 5	6 + 3	6 + 4	7 + 3	8 + 1
2 + 4	6 + 2	4 + 5	7 + 1	8 + 0

Started: _____ Finished: _____ Total Time: _____ Completed: _____ Correct: _____

Name: _____   Date: _____

4 + 4	5 + 5	8 + 2	2 + 3	3 + 4
3 + 3	10 + 0	3 + 2	4 + 3	6 + 4
2 + 2	4 + 5	3 + 6	2 + 4	1 + 3
1 + 1	3 + 5	6 + 0	2 + 8	1 + 8
4 + 6	5 + 2	6 + 2	3 + 6	9 + 1
0 + 0	2 + 1	9 + 0	7 + 3	6 + 3

Started: _____ Finished: _____ Total Time: _____ Completed: _____ Correct: _____

Name: _____   Date: _____

$$
\begin{array}{r} 4 \\ +\,5 \\ \hline \end{array}
\qquad
\begin{array}{r} 9 \\ +\,1 \\ \hline \end{array}
\qquad
\begin{array}{r} 10 \\ +\,0 \\ \hline \end{array}
\qquad
\begin{array}{r} 2 \\ +\,3 \\ \hline \end{array}
\qquad
\begin{array}{r} 8 \\ +\,0 \\ \hline \end{array}
$$

$$
\begin{array}{r} 1 \\ +\,9 \\ \hline \end{array}
\qquad
\begin{array}{r} 6 \\ +\,2 \\ \hline \end{array}
\qquad
\begin{array}{r} 1 \\ +\,3 \\ \hline \end{array}
\qquad
\begin{array}{r} 3 \\ +\,7 \\ \hline \end{array}
\qquad
\begin{array}{r} 0 \\ +\,4 \\ \hline \end{array}
$$

$$
\begin{array}{r} 6 \\ +\,1 \\ \hline \end{array}
\qquad
\begin{array}{r} 2 \\ +\,4 \\ \hline \end{array}
\qquad
\begin{array}{r} 3 \\ +\,3 \\ \hline \end{array}
\qquad
\begin{array}{r} 4 \\ +\,4 \\ \hline \end{array}
\qquad
\begin{array}{r} 1 \\ +\,4 \\ \hline \end{array}
$$

$$
\begin{array}{r} 1 \\ +\,8 \\ \hline \end{array}
\qquad
\begin{array}{r} 5 \\ +\,3 \\ \hline \end{array}
\qquad
\begin{array}{r} 3 \\ +\,5 \\ \hline \end{array}
\qquad
\begin{array}{r} 6 \\ +\,4 \\ \hline \end{array}
\qquad
\begin{array}{r} 0 \\ +\,6 \\ \hline \end{array}
$$

$$
\begin{array}{r} 5 \\ +\,4 \\ \hline \end{array}
\qquad
\begin{array}{r} 7 \\ +\,2 \\ \hline \end{array}
\qquad
\begin{array}{r} 3 \\ +\,4 \\ \hline \end{array}
\qquad
\begin{array}{r} 7 \\ +\,1 \\ \hline \end{array}
\qquad
\begin{array}{r} 8 \\ +\,2 \\ \hline \end{array}
$$

$$
\begin{array}{r} 0 \\ +\,5 \\ \hline \end{array}
\qquad
\begin{array}{r} 5 \\ +\,2 \\ \hline \end{array}
\qquad
\begin{array}{r} 2 \\ +\,6 \\ \hline \end{array}
\qquad
\begin{array}{r} 7 \\ +\,0 \\ \hline \end{array}
\qquad
\begin{array}{r} 4 \\ +\,3 \\ \hline \end{array}
$$

Started: _____   Finished: _____   Total Time: _____   Completed: _____   Correct: _____

Name: _____   Date: _____

$$
\begin{array}{r} 5 \\ +\,2 \\ \hline \end{array}
\qquad
\begin{array}{r} 4 \\ +\,1 \\ \hline \end{array}
\qquad
\begin{array}{r} 3 \\ +\,4 \\ \hline \end{array}
\qquad
\begin{array}{r} 7 \\ +\,1 \\ \hline \end{array}
\qquad
\begin{array}{r} 2 \\ +\,6 \\ \hline \end{array}
$$

$$
\begin{array}{r} 1 \\ +\,9 \\ \hline \end{array}
\qquad
\begin{array}{r} 5 \\ +\,5 \\ \hline \end{array}
\qquad
\begin{array}{r} 6 \\ +\,2 \\ \hline \end{array}
\qquad
\begin{array}{r} 3 \\ +\,7 \\ \hline \end{array}
\qquad
\begin{array}{r} 0 \\ +\,4 \\ \hline \end{array}
$$

$$
\begin{array}{r} 5 \\ +\,4 \\ \hline \end{array}
\qquad
\begin{array}{r} 7 \\ +\,3 \\ \hline \end{array}
\qquad
\begin{array}{r} 7 \\ +\,2 \\ \hline \end{array}
\qquad
\begin{array}{r} 3 \\ +\,6 \\ \hline \end{array}
\qquad
\begin{array}{r} 9 \\ +\,1 \\ \hline \end{array}
$$

$$
\begin{array}{r} 4 \\ +\,2 \\ \hline \end{array}
\qquad
\begin{array}{r} 4 \\ +\,3 \\ \hline \end{array}
\qquad
\begin{array}{r} 4 \\ +\,5 \\ \hline \end{array}
\qquad
\begin{array}{r} 1 \\ +\,6 \\ \hline \end{array}
\qquad
\begin{array}{r} 6 \\ +\,4 \\ \hline \end{array}
$$

$$
\begin{array}{r} 2 \\ +\,2 \\ \hline \end{array}
\qquad
\begin{array}{r} 3 \\ +\,2 \\ \hline \end{array}
\qquad
\begin{array}{r} 8 \\ +\,2 \\ \hline \end{array}
\qquad
\begin{array}{r} 2 \\ +\,4 \\ \hline \end{array}
\qquad
\begin{array}{r} 3 \\ +\,5 \\ \hline \end{array}
$$

$$
\begin{array}{r} 5 \\ +\,3 \\ \hline \end{array}
\qquad
\begin{array}{r} 6 \\ +\,0 \\ \hline \end{array}
\qquad
\begin{array}{r} 2 \\ +\,8 \\ \hline \end{array}
\qquad
\begin{array}{r} 0 \\ +\,5 \\ \hline \end{array}
\qquad
\begin{array}{r} 1 \\ +\,8 \\ \hline \end{array}
$$

Started: _____   Finished: _____   Total Time: _____   Completed: _____   Correct: _____

Name: _____   Date: _____

$$\begin{array}{r} 4 \\ +7 \\ \hline \end{array} \qquad \begin{array}{r} 8 \\ +7 \\ \hline \end{array} \qquad \begin{array}{r} 9 \\ +9 \\ \hline \end{array} \qquad \begin{array}{r} 5 \\ +7 \\ \hline \end{array}$$

$$\begin{array}{r} 8 \\ +3 \\ \hline \end{array} \qquad \begin{array}{r} 9 \\ +8 \\ \hline \end{array} \qquad \begin{array}{r} 7 \\ +4 \\ \hline \end{array} \qquad \begin{array}{r} 6 \\ +6 \\ \hline \end{array}$$

$$\begin{array}{r} 7 \\ +9 \\ \hline \end{array} \qquad \begin{array}{r} 9 \\ +2 \\ \hline \end{array} \qquad \begin{array}{r} 3 \\ +8 \\ \hline \end{array} \qquad \begin{array}{r} 8 \\ +8 \\ \hline \end{array}$$

$$\begin{array}{r} 9 \\ +5 \\ \hline \end{array} \qquad \begin{array}{r} 6 \\ +8 \\ \hline \end{array} \qquad \begin{array}{r} 6 \\ +5 \\ \hline \end{array} \qquad \begin{array}{r} 7 \\ +7 \\ \hline \end{array}$$

$$\begin{array}{r} 5 \\ +6 \\ \hline \end{array} \qquad \begin{array}{r} 4 \\ +9 \\ \hline \end{array} \qquad \begin{array}{r} 7 \\ +5 \\ \hline \end{array} \qquad \begin{array}{r} 7 \\ +8 \\ \hline \end{array}$$

Started: _____   Finished: _____   Total Time: _____   Completed: _____   Correct: _____

Name: _____ Date: _____

$$\begin{array}{r} 5 \\ +9 \\ \hline \end{array} \qquad \begin{array}{r} 9 \\ +4 \\ \hline \end{array} \qquad \begin{array}{r} 8 \\ +5 \\ \hline \end{array} \qquad \begin{array}{r} 9 \\ +6 \\ \hline \end{array}$$

$$\begin{array}{r} 9 \\ +9 \\ \hline \end{array} \qquad \begin{array}{r} 5 \\ +8 \\ \hline \end{array} \qquad \begin{array}{r} 5 \\ +7 \\ \hline \end{array} \qquad \begin{array}{r} 8 \\ +4 \\ \hline \end{array}$$

$$\begin{array}{r} 7 \\ +5 \\ \hline \end{array} \qquad \begin{array}{r} 9 \\ +2 \\ \hline \end{array} \qquad \begin{array}{r} 9 \\ +3 \\ \hline \end{array} \qquad \begin{array}{r} 7 \\ +4 \\ \hline \end{array}$$

$$\begin{array}{r} 9 \\ +5 \\ \hline \end{array} \qquad \begin{array}{r} 6 \\ +8 \\ \hline \end{array} \qquad \begin{array}{r} 5 \\ +6 \\ \hline \end{array} \qquad \begin{array}{r} 6 \\ +9 \\ \hline \end{array}$$

$$\begin{array}{r} 4 \\ +9 \\ \hline \end{array} \qquad \begin{array}{r} 8 \\ +3 \\ \hline \end{array} \qquad \begin{array}{r} 7 \\ +6 \\ \hline \end{array} \qquad \begin{array}{r} 8 \\ +7 \\ \hline \end{array}$$

Started: _____ Finished: _____ Total Time: _____ Completed: _____ Correct: _____

Name: _____   Date: _____

$$\begin{array}{r} 6 \\ +\,7 \\ \hline \end{array}$$ $\qquad$ $$\begin{array}{r} 5 \\ +\,6 \\ \hline \end{array}$$ $\qquad$ $$\begin{array}{r} 4 \\ +\,8 \\ \hline \end{array}$$ $\qquad$ $$\begin{array}{r} 9 \\ +\,3 \\ \hline \end{array}$$

$$\begin{array}{r} 4 \\ +\,9 \\ \hline \end{array}$$ $\qquad$ $$\begin{array}{r} 7 \\ +\,8 \\ \hline \end{array}$$ $\qquad$ $$\begin{array}{r} 7 \\ +\,7 \\ \hline \end{array}$$ $\qquad$ $$\begin{array}{r} 6 \\ +\,8 \\ \hline \end{array}$$

$$\begin{array}{r} 9 \\ +\,5 \\ \hline \end{array}$$ $\qquad$ $$\begin{array}{r} 9 \\ +\,4 \\ \hline \end{array}$$ $\qquad$ $$\begin{array}{r} 9 \\ +\,8 \\ \hline \end{array}$$ $\qquad$ $$\begin{array}{r} 5 \\ +\,9 \\ \hline \end{array}$$

$$\begin{array}{r} 8 \\ +\,5 \\ \hline \end{array}$$ $\qquad$ $$\begin{array}{r} 6 \\ +\,5 \\ \hline \end{array}$$ $\qquad$ $$\begin{array}{r} 7 \\ +\,5 \\ \hline \end{array}$$ $\qquad$ $$\begin{array}{r} 8 \\ +\,7 \\ \hline \end{array}$$

$$\begin{array}{r} 8 \\ +\,4 \\ \hline \end{array}$$ $\qquad$ $$\begin{array}{r} 9 \\ +\,9 \\ \hline \end{array}$$ $\qquad$ $$\begin{array}{r} 7 \\ +\,9 \\ \hline \end{array}$$ $\qquad$ $$\begin{array}{r} 8 \\ +\,3 \\ \hline \end{array}$$

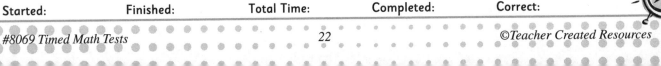

Started: _____   Finished: _____   Total Time: _____   Completed: _____   Correct: _____

Name: _____   Date: _____

$$\begin{array}{r} 6 \\ +\ 7 \\ \hline \end{array} \qquad \begin{array}{r} 9 \\ +\ 9 \\ \hline \end{array} \qquad \begin{array}{r} 4 \\ +\ 8 \\ \hline \end{array} \qquad \begin{array}{r} 7 \\ +\ 4 \\ \hline \end{array}$$

$$\begin{array}{r} 7 \\ +\ 9 \\ \hline \end{array} \qquad \begin{array}{r} 6 \\ +\ 9 \\ \hline \end{array} \qquad \begin{array}{r} 8 \\ +\ 9 \\ \hline \end{array} \qquad \begin{array}{r} 9 \\ +\ 4 \\ \hline \end{array}$$

$$\begin{array}{r} 8 \\ +\ 4 \\ \hline \end{array} \qquad \begin{array}{r} 9 \\ +\ 6 \\ \hline \end{array} \qquad \begin{array}{r} 9 \\ +\ 3 \\ \hline \end{array} \qquad \begin{array}{r} 8 \\ +\ 6 \\ \hline \end{array}$$

$$\begin{array}{r} 7 \\ +\ 5 \\ \hline \end{array} \qquad \begin{array}{r} 6 \\ +\ 8 \\ \hline \end{array} \qquad \begin{array}{r} 7 \\ +\ 6 \\ \hline \end{array} \qquad \begin{array}{r} 8 \\ +\ 8 \\ \hline \end{array}$$

$$\begin{array}{r} 5 \\ +\ 9 \\ \hline \end{array} \qquad \begin{array}{r} 9 \\ +\ 7 \\ \hline \end{array} \qquad \begin{array}{r} 7 \\ +\ 7 \\ \hline \end{array} \qquad \begin{array}{r} 8 \\ +\ 7 \\ \hline \end{array}$$

Started: Finished: Total Time: Completed: Correct:

Name: _____   Date: _____

9 + 2	3 + 8	3 + 9	8 + 4	6 + 5
6 + 6	5 + 9	8 + 5	8 + 8	7 + 7
6 + 8	7 + 9	9 + 4	8 + 3	8 + 9
5 + 7	8 + 5	9 + 7	9 + 9	6 + 7
9 + 3	7 + 8	8 + 6	7 + 5	7 + 6
9 + 6	4 + 7	5 + 6	4 + 9	8 + 7

Started: _____   Finished: _____   Total Time: _____   Completed: _____   Correct: _____

Name: _____   Date: _____

$$\begin{array}{r} 2 \\ +\,9 \\ \hline \end{array} \qquad \begin{array}{r} 7 \\ +\,7 \\ \hline \end{array} \qquad \begin{array}{r} 6 \\ +\,6 \\ \hline \end{array} \qquad \begin{array}{r} 5 \\ +\,8 \\ \hline \end{array} \qquad \begin{array}{r} 9 \\ +\,4 \\ \hline \end{array}$$

$$\begin{array}{r} 4 \\ +\,9 \\ \hline \end{array} \qquad \begin{array}{r} 5 \\ +\,6 \\ \hline \end{array} \qquad \begin{array}{r} 8 \\ +\,8 \\ \hline \end{array} \qquad \begin{array}{r} 7 \\ +\,9 \\ \hline \end{array} \qquad \begin{array}{r} 8 \\ +\,3 \\ \hline \end{array}$$

$$\begin{array}{r} 3 \\ +\,9 \\ \hline \end{array} \qquad \begin{array}{r} 9 \\ +\,8 \\ \hline \end{array} \qquad \begin{array}{r} 9 \\ +\,2 \\ \hline \end{array} \qquad \begin{array}{r} 4 \\ +\,7 \\ \hline \end{array} \qquad \begin{array}{r} 7 \\ +\,6 \\ \hline \end{array}$$

$$\begin{array}{r} 9 \\ +\,6 \\ \hline \end{array} \qquad \begin{array}{r} 8 \\ +\,4 \\ \hline \end{array} \qquad \begin{array}{r} 6 \\ +\,5 \\ \hline \end{array} \qquad \begin{array}{r} 7 \\ +\,8 \\ \hline \end{array} \qquad \begin{array}{r} 6 \\ +\,9 \\ \hline \end{array}$$

$$\begin{array}{r} 9 \\ +\,5 \\ \hline \end{array} \qquad \begin{array}{r} 8 \\ +\,5 \\ \hline \end{array} \qquad \begin{array}{r} 9 \\ +\,9 \\ \hline \end{array} \qquad \begin{array}{r} 7 \\ +\,5 \\ \hline \end{array} \qquad \begin{array}{r} 9 \\ +\,7 \\ \hline \end{array}$$

$$\begin{array}{r} 8 \\ +\,7 \\ \hline \end{array} \qquad \begin{array}{r} 5 \\ +\,9 \\ \hline \end{array} \qquad \begin{array}{r} 3 \\ +\,8 \\ \hline \end{array} \qquad \begin{array}{r} 8 \\ +\,9 \\ \hline \end{array} \qquad \begin{array}{r} 9 \\ +\,3 \\ \hline \end{array}$$

Started: Finished: Total Time: Completed: Correct:

Name: _____   Date: _____

9 + 6	7 + 7	8 + 8	9 + 9	6 + 9
5 + 6	7 + 6	8 + 6	10 + 8	5 + 9
4 + 8	9 + 8	9 + 4	7 + 8	7 + 9
8 + 5	9 + 3	6 + 5	7 + 5	6 + 7
5 + 7	8 + 9	9 + 7	10 + 6	4 + 7
5 + 8	8 + 4	3 + 8	6 + 6	8 + 3

Started: _____   Finished: _____   Total Time: _____   Completed: _____   Correct: _____

Name: _____ Date: _____

$$\begin{array}{r} 8 \\ +\,9 \\ \hline \end{array} \qquad \begin{array}{r} 9 \\ +\,8 \\ \hline \end{array} \qquad \begin{array}{r} 7 \\ +\,4 \\ \hline \end{array} \qquad \begin{array}{r} 7 \\ +\,8 \\ \hline \end{array} \qquad \begin{array}{r} 4 \\ +\,9 \\ \hline \end{array}$$

$$\begin{array}{r} 4 \\ +\,8 \\ \hline \end{array} \qquad \begin{array}{r} 6 \\ +\,7 \\ \hline \end{array} \qquad \begin{array}{r} 9 \\ +\,9 \\ \hline \end{array} \qquad \begin{array}{r} 5 \\ +\,8 \\ \hline \end{array} \qquad \begin{array}{r} 7 \\ +\,5 \\ \hline \end{array}$$

$$\begin{array}{r} 7 \\ +\,9 \\ \hline \end{array} \qquad \begin{array}{r} 8 \\ +\,5 \\ \hline \end{array} \qquad \begin{array}{r} 6 \\ +\,9 \\ \hline \end{array} \qquad \begin{array}{r} 5 \\ +\,7 \\ \hline \end{array} \qquad \begin{array}{r} 9 \\ +\,4 \\ \hline \end{array}$$

$$\begin{array}{r} 8 \\ +\,4 \\ \hline \end{array} \qquad \begin{array}{r} 10 \\ +\,6 \\ \hline \end{array} \qquad \begin{array}{r} 9 \\ +\,3 \\ \hline \end{array} \qquad \begin{array}{r} 8 \\ +\,6 \\ \hline \end{array} \qquad \begin{array}{r} 4 \\ +\,7 \\ \hline \end{array}$$

$$\begin{array}{r} 3 \\ +\,9 \\ \hline \end{array} \qquad \begin{array}{r} 5 \\ +\,6 \\ \hline \end{array} \qquad \begin{array}{r} 6 \\ +\,8 \\ \hline \end{array} \qquad \begin{array}{r} 7 \\ +\,6 \\ \hline \end{array} \qquad \begin{array}{r} 8 \\ +\,8 \\ \hline \end{array}$$

$$\begin{array}{r} 5 \\ +\,9 \\ \hline \end{array} \qquad \begin{array}{r} 9 \\ +\,7 \\ \hline \end{array} \qquad \begin{array}{r} 7 \\ +\,7 \\ \hline \end{array} \qquad \begin{array}{r} 10 \\ +\,7 \\ \hline \end{array} \qquad \begin{array}{r} 9 \\ +\,5 \\ \hline \end{array}$$

Started: _____ Finished: _____ Total Time: _____ Completed: _____ Correct: _____

Name: _____   Date: _____

$$\begin{array}{r} 5 \\ +\,9 \\ \hline \end{array} \qquad \begin{array}{r} 8 \\ +\,3 \\ \hline \end{array} \qquad \begin{array}{r} 4 \\ +\,7 \\ \hline \end{array} \qquad \begin{array}{r} 6 \\ +\,5 \\ \hline \end{array}$$

$$\begin{array}{r} 10 \\ +\,2 \\ \hline \end{array} \qquad \begin{array}{r} 8 \\ +\,4 \\ \hline \end{array} \qquad \begin{array}{r} 6 \\ +\,7 \\ \hline \end{array} \qquad \begin{array}{r} 9 \\ +\,5 \\ \hline \end{array}$$

$$\begin{array}{r} 9 \\ +\,9 \\ \hline \end{array} \qquad \begin{array}{r} 8 \\ +\,9 \\ \hline \end{array} \qquad \begin{array}{r} 11 \\ +\,9 \\ \hline \end{array} \qquad \begin{array}{r} 9 \\ +\,6 \\ \hline \end{array}$$

$$\begin{array}{r} 7 \\ +\,7 \\ \hline \end{array} \qquad \begin{array}{r} 7 \\ +\,8 \\ \hline \end{array} \qquad \begin{array}{r} 8 \\ +\,8 \\ \hline \end{array} \qquad \begin{array}{r} 9 \\ +\,4 \\ \hline \end{array}$$

$$\begin{array}{r} 10 \\ +\,10 \\ \hline \end{array} \qquad \begin{array}{r} 6 \\ +\,9 \\ \hline \end{array} \qquad \begin{array}{r} 5 \\ +\,8 \\ \hline \end{array} \qquad \begin{array}{r} 10 \\ +\,8 \\ \hline \end{array}$$

Started: _____ Finished: _____ Total Time: _____ Completed: _____ Correct: _____

Name: _____   Date: _____

9 + 7	8 + 7	9 + 9	5 + 7
8 + 3	8 + 8	7 + 4	6 + 6
7 + 9	9 + 2	10 + 3	8 + 6
9 + 5	10 + 10	6 + 5	7 + 7
10 + 9	4 + 9	7 + 5	7 + 8

Started: _____   Finished: _____   Total Time: _____   Completed: _____   Correct: _____

Name: _____   Date: _____

10 + 9	8 + 5	6 + 9	7 + 7	9 + 4
8 + 4	10 + 6	9 + 3	8 + 6	4 + 7
8 + 9	9 + 8	7 + 5	7 + 8	4 + 9
10 + 10	6 + 7	9 + 9	5 + 8	7 + 4
3 + 9	6 + 6	6 + 8	7 + 6	8 + 8
4 + 8	9 + 7	5 + 7	10 + 7	9 + 5

Started: Finished: Total Time: Completed: Correct:

Name: _____   Date: _____

10 + 10	5 + 6	6 + 8	7 + 6	8 + 8
9 + 5	5 + 8	10 + 9	7 + 5	7 + 7
8 + 7	9 + 9	3 + 8	8 + 9	9 + 3
4 + 8	9 + 8	9 + 4	7 + 8	7 + 9
8 + 5	9 + 3	6 + 6	6 + 5	6 + 7
8 + 6	9 + 7	5 + 7	10 + 7	5 + 9

Started: Finished: Total Time: Completed: Correct:

Name: _____ Date: _____

$$1 + 3$$ $$3 + 5$$ $$5 + 7$$ $$7 + 2$$

$$2 + 3$$ $$4 + 5$$ $$6 + 7$$ $$8 + 2$$

$$9 + 3$$ $$3 + 2$$ $$6 + 6$$ $$7 + 8$$

$$6 + 3$$ $$8 + 9$$ $$4 + 7$$ $$2 + 2$$

$$1 + 8$$ $$2 + 5$$ $$7 + 7$$ $$7 + 3$$

Started: Finished: Total Time: Completed: Correct:

Name: _____   Date: _____

$$\begin{array}{r} 2 \\ +\,3 \\ \hline \end{array} \qquad \begin{array}{r} 4 \\ +\,5 \\ \hline \end{array} \qquad \begin{array}{r} 6 \\ +\,7 \\ \hline \end{array} \qquad \begin{array}{r} 8 \\ +\,2 \\ \hline \end{array}$$

$$\begin{array}{r} 8 \\ +\,3 \\ \hline \end{array} \qquad \begin{array}{r} 8 \\ +\,8 \\ \hline \end{array} \qquad \begin{array}{r} 4 \\ +\,7 \\ \hline \end{array} \qquad \begin{array}{r} 2 \\ +\,2 \\ \hline \end{array}$$

$$\begin{array}{r} 7 \\ +\,3 \\ \hline \end{array} \qquad \begin{array}{r} 1 \\ +\,2 \\ \hline \end{array} \qquad \begin{array}{r} 4 \\ +\,6 \\ \hline \end{array} \qquad \begin{array}{r} 5 \\ +\,8 \\ \hline \end{array}$$

$$\begin{array}{r} 4 \\ +\,3 \\ \hline \end{array} \qquad \begin{array}{r} 5 \\ +\,5 \\ \hline \end{array} \qquad \begin{array}{r} 2 \\ +\,7 \\ \hline \end{array} \qquad \begin{array}{r} 0 \\ +\,2 \\ \hline \end{array}$$

$$\begin{array}{r} 0 \\ +\,8 \\ \hline \end{array} \qquad \begin{array}{r} 1 \\ +\,5 \\ \hline \end{array} \qquad \begin{array}{r} 9 \\ +\,9 \\ \hline \end{array} \qquad \begin{array}{r} 5 \\ +\,3 \\ \hline \end{array}$$

Started: Finished: Total Time: Completed: Correct:

Name: _____   Date: _____

$$
\begin{array}{r} 7 \\ +5 \\ \hline \end{array}
\qquad
\begin{array}{r} 1 \\ +4 \\ \hline \end{array}
\qquad
\begin{array}{r} 4 \\ +8 \\ \hline \end{array}
\qquad
\begin{array}{r} 5 \\ +9 \\ \hline \end{array}
$$

$$
\begin{array}{r} 4 \\ +5 \\ \hline \end{array}
\qquad
\begin{array}{r} 5 \\ +7 \\ \hline \end{array}
\qquad
\begin{array}{r} 2 \\ +9 \\ \hline \end{array}
\qquad
\begin{array}{r} 0 \\ +4 \\ \hline \end{array}
$$

$$
\begin{array}{r} 3 \\ +9 \\ \hline \end{array}
\qquad
\begin{array}{r} 1 \\ +7 \\ \hline \end{array}
\qquad
\begin{array}{r} 2 \\ +8 \\ \hline \end{array}
\qquad
\begin{array}{r} 5 \\ +5 \\ \hline \end{array}
$$

$$
\begin{array}{r} 2 \\ +5 \\ \hline \end{array}
\qquad
\begin{array}{r} 4 \\ +7 \\ \hline \end{array}
\qquad
\begin{array}{r} 6 \\ +9 \\ \hline \end{array}
\qquad
\begin{array}{r} 8 \\ +9 \\ \hline \end{array}
$$

$$
\begin{array}{r} 8 \\ +5 \\ \hline \end{array}
\qquad
\begin{array}{r} 2 \\ +3 \\ \hline \end{array}
\qquad
\begin{array}{r} 4 \\ +9 \\ \hline \end{array}
\qquad
\begin{array}{r} 9 \\ +7 \\ \hline \end{array}
$$

Started: Finished: Total Time: Completed: Correct:

Name: _____   Date: _____

$$
\begin{array}{r} 2 \\ +\,4 \\ \hline \end{array}
\qquad
\begin{array}{r} 10 \\ +\,6 \\ \hline \end{array}
\qquad
\begin{array}{r} 7 \\ +\,3 \\ \hline \end{array}
\qquad
\begin{array}{r} 5 \\ +\,6 \\ \hline \end{array}
$$

$$
\begin{array}{r} 7 \\ +\,7 \\ \hline \end{array}
\qquad
\begin{array}{r} 9 \\ +\,9 \\ \hline \end{array}
\qquad
\begin{array}{r} 4 \\ +\,4 \\ \hline \end{array}
\qquad
\begin{array}{r} 8 \\ +\,8 \\ \hline \end{array}
$$

$$
\begin{array}{r} 7 \\ +\,9 \\ \hline \end{array}
\qquad
\begin{array}{r} 4 \\ +\,9 \\ \hline \end{array}
\qquad
\begin{array}{r} 10 \\ +\,9 \\ \hline \end{array}
\qquad
\begin{array}{r} 5 \\ +\,4 \\ \hline \end{array}
$$

$$
\begin{array}{r} 7 \\ +\,5 \\ \hline \end{array}
\qquad
\begin{array}{r} 6 \\ +\,8 \\ \hline \end{array}
\qquad
\begin{array}{r} 7 \\ +\,6 \\ \hline \end{array}
\qquad
\begin{array}{r} 3 \\ +\,8 \\ \hline \end{array}
$$

$$
\begin{array}{r} 5 \\ +\,5 \\ \hline \end{array}
\qquad
\begin{array}{r} 9 \\ +\,7 \\ \hline \end{array}
\qquad
\begin{array}{r} 10 \\ +\,7 \\ \hline \end{array}
\qquad
\begin{array}{r} 2 \\ +\,7 \\ \hline \end{array}
$$

Started: Finished: Total Time: Completed: Correct:

Name: _____   Date: _____

10 + 9	9 + 8	2 + 4	7 + 8	3 + 9
2 + 8	6 + 0	9 + 1	5 + 8	10 + 5
7 + 1	3 + 5	6 + 9	5 + 0	9 + 2
3 + 4	2 + 6	3 + 3	8 + 1	4 + 7
6 + 6	5 + 5	6 + 2	7 + 6	8 + 2
9 + 9	10 + 7	7 + 7	8 + 3	4 + 5

Started: Finished: Total Time: Completed: Correct:

Name: _____   Date: _____

$$\begin{array}{r} 5 \\ +8 \\ \hline \end{array} \quad \begin{array}{r} 6 \\ +0 \\ \hline \end{array} \quad \begin{array}{r} 9 \\ +1 \\ \hline \end{array} \quad \begin{array}{r} 2 \\ +2 \\ \hline \end{array} \quad \begin{array}{r} 3 \\ +5 \\ \hline \end{array}$$

$$\begin{array}{r} 10 \\ +9 \\ \hline \end{array} \quad \begin{array}{r} 6 \\ +8 \\ \hline \end{array} \quad \begin{array}{r} 2 \\ +4 \\ \hline \end{array} \quad \begin{array}{r} 2 \\ +8 \\ \hline \end{array} \quad \begin{array}{r} 3 \\ +9 \\ \hline \end{array}$$

$$\begin{array}{r} 7 \\ +1 \\ \hline \end{array} \quad \begin{array}{r} 1 \\ +5 \\ \hline \end{array} \quad \begin{array}{r} 7 \\ +9 \\ \hline \end{array} \quad \begin{array}{r} 5 \\ +0 \\ \hline \end{array} \quad \begin{array}{r} 9 \\ +2 \\ \hline \end{array}$$

$$\begin{array}{r} 8 \\ +9 \\ \hline \end{array} \quad \begin{array}{r} 5 \\ +4 \\ \hline \end{array} \quad \begin{array}{r} 6 \\ +2 \\ \hline \end{array} \quad \begin{array}{r} 8 \\ +6 \\ \hline \end{array} \quad \begin{array}{r} 8 \\ +2 \\ \hline \end{array}$$

$$\begin{array}{r} 9 \\ +9 \\ \hline \end{array} \quad \begin{array}{r} 10 \\ +7 \\ \hline \end{array} \quad \begin{array}{r} 7 \\ +7 \\ \hline \end{array} \quad \begin{array}{r} 8 \\ +3 \\ \hline \end{array} \quad \begin{array}{r} 9 \\ +5 \\ \hline \end{array}$$

$$\begin{array}{r} 10 \\ +10 \\ \hline \end{array} \quad \begin{array}{r} 2 \\ +6 \\ \hline \end{array} \quad \begin{array}{r} 3 \\ +3 \\ \hline \end{array} \quad \begin{array}{r} 8 \\ +1 \\ \hline \end{array} \quad \begin{array}{r} 4 \\ +7 \\ \hline \end{array}$$

Started: Finished: Total Time: Completed: Correct:

Name: _____   Date: _____

3 + 7	4 + 1	9 + 2	4 + 3	5 + 8
9 + 0	8 + 9	6 + 2	3 + 3	7 + 4
8 + 7	5 + 2	9 + 7	9 + 4	9 + 9
10 + 9	7 + 2	3 + 8	2 + 7	5 + 9
5 + 7	6 + 9	6 + 4	9 + 3	8 + 4
10 + 10	5 + 4	4 + 6	7 + 0	8 + 5

Started: _____   Finished: _____   Total Time: _____   Completed: _____   Correct: _____

Name: _____   Date: _____

$$
\begin{array}{r} 3 \\ +\,4 \\ \hline \end{array}
\qquad
\begin{array}{r} 9 \\ +\,0 \\ \hline \end{array}
\qquad
\begin{array}{r} 3 \\ +\,5 \\ \hline \end{array}
\qquad
\begin{array}{r} 6 \\ +\,3 \\ \hline \end{array}
\qquad
\begin{array}{r} 6 \\ +\,9 \\ \hline \end{array}
$$

$$
\begin{array}{r} 6 \\ +\,4 \\ \hline \end{array}
\qquad
\begin{array}{r} 10 \\ +\,9 \\ \hline \end{array}
\qquad
\begin{array}{r} 2 \\ +\,3 \\ \hline \end{array}
\qquad
\begin{array}{r} 8 \\ +\,8 \\ \hline \end{array}
\qquad
\begin{array}{r} 3 \\ +\,7 \\ \hline \end{array}
$$

$$
\begin{array}{r} 6 \\ +\,2 \\ \hline \end{array}
\qquad
\begin{array}{r} 4 \\ +\,4 \\ \hline \end{array}
\qquad
\begin{array}{r} 3 \\ +\,6 \\ \hline \end{array}
\qquad
\begin{array}{r} 8 \\ +\,4 \\ \hline \end{array}
\qquad
\begin{array}{r} 5 \\ +\,3 \\ \hline \end{array}
$$

$$
\begin{array}{r} 1 \\ +\,6 \\ \hline \end{array}
\qquad
\begin{array}{r} 8 \\ +\,5 \\ \hline \end{array}
\qquad
\begin{array}{r} 6 \\ +\,7 \\ \hline \end{array}
\qquad
\begin{array}{r} 8 \\ +\,2 \\ \hline \end{array}
\qquad
\begin{array}{r} 1 \\ +\,8 \\ \hline \end{array}
$$

$$
\begin{array}{r} 4 \\ +\,6 \\ \hline \end{array}
\qquad
\begin{array}{r} 2 \\ +\,2 \\ \hline \end{array}
\qquad
\begin{array}{r} 6 \\ +\,5 \\ \hline \end{array}
\qquad
\begin{array}{r} 0 \\ +\,6 \\ \hline \end{array}
\qquad
\begin{array}{r} 9 \\ +\,8 \\ \hline \end{array}
$$

$$
\begin{array}{r} 9 \\ +\,9 \\ \hline \end{array}
\qquad
\begin{array}{r} 2 \\ +\,6 \\ \hline \end{array}
\qquad
\begin{array}{r} 7 \\ +\,0 \\ \hline \end{array}
\qquad
\begin{array}{r} 9 \\ +\,3 \\ \hline \end{array}
\qquad
\begin{array}{r} 7 \\ +\,6 \\ \hline \end{array}
$$

Started: Finished: Total Time: Completed: Correct:

Name: _____   Date: _____

7 $+\,2$	4 $+\,4$	3 $+\,6$	8 $+\,4$	5 $+\,3$
4 $+\,5$	9 $+\,4$	9 $+\,0$	2 $+\,3$	8 $+\,0$
8 $+\,9$	6 $+\,2$	1 $+\,3$	5 $+\,7$	0 $+\,4$
8 $+\,1$	2 $+\,4$	6 $+\,6$	7 $+\,4$	1 $+\,8$
6 $+\,9$	3 $+\,5$	9 $+\,9$	3 $+\,7$	0 $+\,6$
5 $+\,4$	7 $+\,3$	3 $+\,4$	7 $+\,9$	7 $+\,2$
5 $+\,5$	9 $+\,1$	8 $+\,8$	3 $+\,3$	3 $+\,0$
10 $+\,10$	6 $+\,8$	9 $+\,3$	7 $+\,7$	5 $+\,0$

Started: Finished: Total Time: Completed: Correct:

Name: _____   Date: _____

10 +9	9 +6	1 +1	8 +8	9 +9
0 +9	2 +9	7 +9	6 +7	4 +7
5 +6	9 +0	7 +6	8 +6	10 +1
8 +9	4 +5	9 +8	9 +4	7 +8
2 +5	9 +3	10 +5	9 +7	7 +5
5 +7	3 +5	6 +6	8 +0	10 +9
2 +3	5 +8	8 +4	3 +8	8 +5
8 +3	5 +5	4 +3	7 +7	2 +1

Started: _____ Finished: _____ Total Time: _____ Completed: _____ Correct: _____

Name: _____   Date: _____

9 + 8	7 + 9	6 + 6	8 + 5	1 + 3
1 + 6	8 + 4	9 + 5	10 + 9	2 + 9
8 + 9	8 + 6	9 + 6	1 + 9	5 + 9
8 + 8	4 + 8	3 + 1	9 + 4	7 + 8
9 + 3	6 + 5	9 + 7	7 + 5	2 + 5
5 + 7	6 + 9	8 + 7	3 + 9	4 + 7
5 + 3	6 + 8	3 + 4	5 + 8	4 + 9
9 + 9	3 + 8	6 + 7	7 + 7	6 + 4

Started: _____   Finished: _____   Total Time: _____   Completed: _____   Correct: _____

Name: _____   Date: _____

$$
\begin{array}{r} 0 \\ +\,9 \\ \hline \end{array}
\qquad
\begin{array}{r} 2 \\ +\,9 \\ \hline \end{array}
\qquad
\begin{array}{r} 7 \\ +\,9 \\ \hline \end{array}
\qquad
\begin{array}{r} 6 \\ +\,7 \\ \hline \end{array}
\qquad
\begin{array}{r} 4 \\ +\,7 \\ \hline \end{array}
$$

$$
\begin{array}{r} 8 \\ +\,9 \\ \hline \end{array}
\qquad
\begin{array}{r} 4 \\ +\,8 \\ \hline \end{array}
\qquad
\begin{array}{r} 9 \\ +\,8 \\ \hline \end{array}
\qquad
\begin{array}{r} 9 \\ +\,4 \\ \hline \end{array}
\qquad
\begin{array}{r} 7 \\ +\,8 \\ \hline \end{array}
$$

$$
\begin{array}{r} 5 \\ +\,4 \\ \hline \end{array}
\qquad
\begin{array}{r} 7 \\ +\,6 \\ \hline \end{array}
\qquad
\begin{array}{r} 7 \\ +\,2 \\ \hline \end{array}
\qquad
\begin{array}{r} 3 \\ +\,6 \\ \hline \end{array}
\qquad
\begin{array}{r} 9 \\ +\,1 \\ \hline \end{array}
$$

$$
\begin{array}{r} 7 \\ +\,0 \\ \hline \end{array}
\qquad
\begin{array}{r} 5 \\ +\,6 \\ \hline \end{array}
\qquad
\begin{array}{r} 8 \\ +\,7 \\ \hline \end{array}
\qquad
\begin{array}{r} 10 \\ +\,7 \\ \hline \end{array}
\qquad
\begin{array}{r} 7 \\ +\,3 \\ \hline \end{array}
$$

$$
\begin{array}{r} 10 \\ +\,9 \\ \hline \end{array}
\qquad
\begin{array}{r} 9 \\ +\,6 \\ \hline \end{array}
\qquad
\begin{array}{r} 1 \\ +\,1 \\ \hline \end{array}
\qquad
\begin{array}{r} 8 \\ +\,8 \\ \hline \end{array}
\qquad
\begin{array}{r} 9 \\ +\,9 \\ \hline \end{array}
$$

$$
\begin{array}{r} 2 \\ +\,5 \\ \hline \end{array}
\qquad
\begin{array}{r} 9 \\ +\,3 \\ \hline \end{array}
\qquad
\begin{array}{r} 10 \\ +\,5 \\ \hline \end{array}
\qquad
\begin{array}{r} 9 \\ +\,7 \\ \hline \end{array}
\qquad
\begin{array}{r} 7 \\ +\,5 \\ \hline \end{array}
$$

$$
\begin{array}{r} 5 \\ +\,7 \\ \hline \end{array}
\qquad
\begin{array}{r} 8 \\ +\,9 \\ \hline \end{array}
\qquad
\begin{array}{r} 8 \\ +\,7 \\ \hline \end{array}
\qquad
\begin{array}{r} 10 \\ +\,8 \\ \hline \end{array}
\qquad
\begin{array}{r} 4 \\ +\,7 \\ \hline \end{array}
$$

$$
\begin{array}{r} 1 \\ +\,4 \\ \hline \end{array}
\qquad
\begin{array}{r} 5 \\ +\,5 \\ \hline \end{array}
\qquad
\begin{array}{r} 6 \\ +\,3 \\ \hline \end{array}
\qquad
\begin{array}{r} 4 \\ +\,9 \\ \hline \end{array}
\qquad
\begin{array}{r} 8 \\ +\,1 \\ \hline \end{array}
$$

Started: _____   Finished: _____   Total Time: _____   Completed: _____   Correct: _____

Name: _____   Date: _____

$$\begin{array}{r} 0 \\ +\ 8 \\ \hline \end{array} \qquad \begin{array}{r} 1 \\ +\ 9 \\ \hline \end{array} \qquad \begin{array}{r} 7 \\ +\ 8 \\ \hline \end{array} \qquad \begin{array}{r} 7 \\ +\ 7 \\ \hline \end{array} \qquad \begin{array}{r} 4 \\ +\ 5 \\ \hline \end{array}$$

$$\begin{array}{r} 9 \\ +\ 9 \\ \hline \end{array} \qquad \begin{array}{r} 4 \\ +\ 7 \\ \hline \end{array} \qquad \begin{array}{r} 8 \\ +\ 8 \\ \hline \end{array} \qquad \begin{array}{r} 9 \\ +\ 3 \\ \hline \end{array} \qquad \begin{array}{r} 6 \\ +\ 8 \\ \hline \end{array}$$

$$\begin{array}{r} 6 \\ +\ 4 \\ \hline \end{array} \qquad \begin{array}{r} 7 \\ +\ 2 \\ \hline \end{array} \qquad \begin{array}{r} 5 \\ +\ 2 \\ \hline \end{array} \qquad \begin{array}{r} 9 \\ +\ 6 \\ \hline \end{array} \qquad \begin{array}{r} 9 \\ +\ 1 \\ \hline \end{array}$$

$$\begin{array}{r} 8 \\ +\ 9 \\ \hline \end{array} \qquad \begin{array}{r} 5 \\ +\ 5 \\ \hline \end{array} \qquad \begin{array}{r} 9 \\ +\ 7 \\ \hline \end{array} \qquad \begin{array}{r} 1 \\ +\ 5 \\ \hline \end{array} \qquad \begin{array}{r} 8 \\ +\ 3 \\ \hline \end{array}$$

$$\begin{array}{r} 10 \\ +\ 8 \\ \hline \end{array} \qquad \begin{array}{r} 8 \\ +\ 6 \\ \hline \end{array} \qquad \begin{array}{r} 2 \\ +\ 1 \\ \hline \end{array} \qquad \begin{array}{r} 9 \\ +\ 8 \\ \hline \end{array} \qquad \begin{array}{r} 5 \\ +\ 9 \\ \hline \end{array}$$

$$\begin{array}{r} 2 \\ +\ 4 \\ \hline \end{array} \qquad \begin{array}{r} 5 \\ +\ 3 \\ \hline \end{array} \qquad \begin{array}{r} 8 \\ +\ 5 \\ \hline \end{array} \qquad \begin{array}{r} 10 \\ +\ 9 \\ \hline \end{array} \qquad \begin{array}{r} 7 \\ +\ 5 \\ \hline \end{array}$$

$$\begin{array}{r} 6 \\ +\ 7 \\ \hline \end{array} \qquad \begin{array}{r} 7 \\ +\ 9 \\ \hline \end{array} \qquad \begin{array}{r} 3 \\ +\ 7 \\ \hline \end{array} \qquad \begin{array}{r} 0 \\ +\ 9 \\ \hline \end{array} \qquad \begin{array}{r} 4 \\ +\ 1 \\ \hline \end{array}$$

$$\begin{array}{r} 3 \\ +\ 4 \\ \hline \end{array} \qquad \begin{array}{r} 5 \\ +\ 0 \\ \hline \end{array} \qquad \begin{array}{r} 6 \\ +\ 3 \\ \hline \end{array} \qquad \begin{array}{r} 7 \\ +\ 3 \\ \hline \end{array} \qquad \begin{array}{r} 8 \\ +\ 1 \\ \hline \end{array}$$

$$\begin{array}{r} 9 \\ +\ 3 \\ \hline \end{array} \qquad \begin{array}{r} 3 \\ +\ 5 \\ \hline \end{array} \qquad \begin{array}{r} 1 \\ +\ 3 \\ \hline \end{array} \qquad \begin{array}{r} 8 \\ +\ 3 \\ \hline \end{array} \qquad \begin{array}{r} 5 \\ +\ 6 \\ \hline \end{array}$$

$$\begin{array}{r} 10 \\ +\ 1 \\ \hline \end{array} \qquad \begin{array}{r} 6 \\ +\ 2 \\ \hline \end{array} \qquad \begin{array}{r} 7 \\ +\ 0 \\ \hline \end{array} \qquad \begin{array}{r} 0 \\ +\ 0 \\ \hline \end{array} \qquad \begin{array}{r} 10 \\ +\ 10 \\ \hline \end{array}$$

Started: _____   Finished: _____   Total Time: _____   Completed: _____   Correct: _____

Name: _____ Date: _____

$$\begin{array}{r} 2 \\ +8 \\ \hline \end{array} \qquad \begin{array}{r} 1 \\ +9 \\ \hline \end{array} \qquad \begin{array}{r} 8 \\ +8 \\ \hline \end{array} \qquad \begin{array}{r} 7 \\ +7 \\ \hline \end{array} \qquad \begin{array}{r} 10 \\ +5 \\ \hline \end{array}$$

$$\begin{array}{r} 10 \\ +9 \\ \hline \end{array} \qquad \begin{array}{r} 5 \\ +6 \\ \hline \end{array} \qquad \begin{array}{r} 8 \\ +5 \\ \hline \end{array} \qquad \begin{array}{r} 9 \\ +1 \\ \hline \end{array} \qquad \begin{array}{r} 7 \\ +5 \\ \hline \end{array}$$

$$\begin{array}{r} 9 \\ +8 \\ \hline \end{array} \qquad \begin{array}{r} 4 \\ +9 \\ \hline \end{array} \qquad \begin{array}{r} 8 \\ +7 \\ \hline \end{array} \qquad \begin{array}{r} 7 \\ +8 \\ \hline \end{array} \qquad \begin{array}{r} 6 \\ +3 \\ \hline \end{array}$$

$$\begin{array}{r} 5 \\ +8 \\ \hline \end{array} \qquad \begin{array}{r} 10 \\ +3 \\ \hline \end{array} \qquad \begin{array}{r} 6 \\ +5 \\ \hline \end{array} \qquad \begin{array}{r} 3 \\ +7 \\ \hline \end{array} \qquad \begin{array}{r} 9 \\ +5 \\ \hline \end{array}$$

$$\begin{array}{r} 1 \\ +8 \\ \hline \end{array} \qquad \begin{array}{r} 7 \\ +9 \\ \hline \end{array} \qquad \begin{array}{r} 6 \\ +8 \\ \hline \end{array} \qquad \begin{array}{r} 4 \\ +7 \\ \hline \end{array} \qquad \begin{array}{r} 5 \\ +5 \\ \hline \end{array}$$

$$\begin{array}{r} 6 \\ +4 \\ \hline \end{array} \qquad \begin{array}{r} 4 \\ +8 \\ \hline \end{array} \qquad \begin{array}{r} 8 \\ +4 \\ \hline \end{array} \qquad \begin{array}{r} 9 \\ +2 \\ \hline \end{array} \qquad \begin{array}{r} 6 \\ +9 \\ \hline \end{array}$$

$$\begin{array}{r} 9 \\ +9 \\ \hline \end{array} \qquad \begin{array}{r} 10 \\ +9 \\ \hline \end{array} \qquad \begin{array}{r} 8 \\ +3 \\ \hline \end{array} \qquad \begin{array}{r} 9 \\ +3 \\ \hline \end{array} \qquad \begin{array}{r} 10 \\ +8 \\ \hline \end{array}$$

$$\begin{array}{r} 9 \\ +0 \\ \hline \end{array} \qquad \begin{array}{r} 3 \\ +8 \\ \hline \end{array} \qquad \begin{array}{r} 4 \\ +5 \\ \hline \end{array} \qquad \begin{array}{r} 6 \\ +7 \\ \hline \end{array} \qquad \begin{array}{r} 8 \\ +9 \\ \hline \end{array}$$

$$\begin{array}{r} 10 \\ +10 \\ \hline \end{array} \qquad \begin{array}{r} 7 \\ +6 \\ \hline \end{array} \qquad \begin{array}{r} 3 \\ +5 \\ \hline \end{array} \qquad \begin{array}{r} 5 \\ +7 \\ \hline \end{array} \qquad \begin{array}{r} 3 \\ +9 \\ \hline \end{array}$$

$$\begin{array}{r} 4 \\ +4 \\ \hline \end{array} \qquad \begin{array}{r} 6 \\ +6 \\ \hline \end{array} \qquad \begin{array}{r} 5 \\ +4 \\ \hline \end{array} \qquad \begin{array}{r} 3 \\ +6 \\ \hline \end{array} \qquad \begin{array}{r} 5 \\ +9 \\ \hline \end{array}$$

Started: _____ Finished: _____ Total Time: _____ Completed: _____ Correct: _____

Name: _____   Date: _____

6 + 4	7 + 2	5 + 2	9 + 6	2 + 9
8 + 9	5 + 5	9 + 7	1 + 5	8 + 3
10 + 8	8 + 6	2 + 1	9 + 8	5 + 9
2 + 4	5 + 3	10 + 5	9 + 1	7 + 5
6 + 7	8 + 8	3 + 7	0 + 9	4 + 1
1 + 4	5 + 0	6 + 3	7 + 3	8 + 1
3 + 9	3 + 5	1 + 3	4 + 5	5 + 2
10 + 1	6 + 2	7 + 0	10 + 10	8 + 5
2 + 5	9 + 3	6 + 5	6 + 9	6 + 6
7 + 6	5 + 9	10 + 9	2 + 6	9 + 9

Started: _____   Finished: _____   Total Time: _____   Completed: _____   Correct: _____

Name: _____   Date: _____

2 + 4	6 + 0	7 + 3	8 + 3	9 + 4
8 + 2	2 + 5	1 + 3	4 + 5	5 + 2
9 + 7	6 + 5	8 + 0	10 + 1	7 + 7
9 + 5	10 + 3	6 + 6	8 + 7	5 + 5
7 + 4	10 + 10	10 + 9	3 + 6	9 + 9
6 + 4	6 + 2	10 + 2	8 + 6	6 + 1
8 + 8	4 + 4	10 + 7	3 + 5	8 + 1
10 + 8	8 + 4	2 + 1	9 + 8	5 + 9
6 + 9	5 + 6	8 + 5	9 + 1	7 + 5
6 + 7	10 + 4	7 + 2	10 + 5	4 + 0

Started: _____   Finished: _____   Total Time: _____   Completed: _____   Correct: _____

Name: _____   Date: _____

8 − 3	8 − 2	7 − 0	5 − 0
4 − 4	5 − 3	2 − 2	1 − 0
10 − 7	9 − 6	8 − 7	7 − 6
5 − 4	6 − 3	3 − 2	4 − 0
9 − 4	0 − 0	6 − 4	5 − 2

Started: _____   Finished: _____   Total Time: _____   Completed: _____   Correct: _____

Name: _____   Date: _____

$$\begin{array}{r} 8 \\ -5 \\ \hline \end{array} \qquad \begin{array}{r} 9 \\ -3 \\ \hline \end{array} \qquad \begin{array}{r} 6 \\ -2 \\ \hline \end{array} \qquad \begin{array}{r} 5 \\ -0 \\ \hline \end{array}$$

$$\begin{array}{r} 2 \\ -0 \\ \hline \end{array} \qquad \begin{array}{r} 10 \\ -9 \\ \hline \end{array} \qquad \begin{array}{r} 9 \\ -0 \\ \hline \end{array} \qquad \begin{array}{r} 9 \\ -6 \\ \hline \end{array}$$

$$\begin{array}{r} 2 \\ -1 \\ \hline \end{array} \qquad \begin{array}{r} 4 \\ -2 \\ \hline \end{array} \qquad \begin{array}{r} 6 \\ -3 \\ \hline \end{array} \qquad \begin{array}{r} 8 \\ -4 \\ \hline \end{array}$$

$$\begin{array}{r} 7 \\ -4 \\ \hline \end{array} \qquad \begin{array}{r} 5 \\ -3 \\ \hline \end{array} \qquad \begin{array}{r} 8 \\ -2 \\ \hline \end{array} \qquad \begin{array}{r} 10 \\ -0 \\ \hline \end{array}$$

$$\begin{array}{r} 6 \\ -4 \\ \hline \end{array} \qquad \begin{array}{r} 10 \\ -3 \\ \hline \end{array} \qquad \begin{array}{r} 2 \\ -2 \\ \hline \end{array} \qquad \begin{array}{r} 5 \\ -4 \\ \hline \end{array}$$

Started: _____ Finished: _____ Total Time: _____ Completed: _____ Correct: _____

Name: _____   Date: _____

$$\begin{array}{r} 10 \\ -\ 6 \\ \hline \end{array} \qquad \begin{array}{r} 9 \\ -\ 9 \\ \hline \end{array} \qquad \begin{array}{r} 3 \\ -\ 0 \\ \hline \end{array} \qquad \begin{array}{r} 9 \\ -\ 4 \\ \hline \end{array}$$

$$\begin{array}{r} 8 \\ -\ 1 \\ \hline \end{array} \qquad \begin{array}{r} 6 \\ -\ 6 \\ \hline \end{array} \qquad \begin{array}{r} 7 \\ -\ 7 \\ \hline \end{array} \qquad \begin{array}{r} 5 \\ -\ 4 \\ \hline \end{array}$$

$$\begin{array}{r} 7 \\ -\ 1 \\ \hline \end{array} \qquad \begin{array}{r} 8 \\ -\ 4 \\ \hline \end{array} \qquad \begin{array}{r} 6 \\ -\ 3 \\ \hline \end{array} \qquad \begin{array}{r} 9 \\ -\ 8 \\ \hline \end{array}$$

$$\begin{array}{r} 5 \\ -\ 2 \\ \hline \end{array} \qquad \begin{array}{r} 6 \\ -\ 5 \\ \hline \end{array} \qquad \begin{array}{r} 8 \\ -\ 8 \\ \hline \end{array} \qquad \begin{array}{r} 10 \\ -\ 4 \\ \hline \end{array}$$

$$\begin{array}{r} 6 \\ -\ 4 \\ \hline \end{array} \qquad \begin{array}{r} 10 \\ -\ 2 \\ \hline \end{array} \qquad \begin{array}{r} 8 \\ -\ 2 \\ \hline \end{array} \qquad \begin{array}{r} 9 \\ -\ 0 \\ \hline \end{array}$$

Started: _____   Finished: _____   Total Time: _____   Completed: _____   Correct: _____

Name: _____   Date: _____

10 − 7	8 − 6	9 − 6	2 − 0
10 − 5	4 − 1	7 − 3	8 − 7
8 − 3	10 − 6	9 − 7	5 − 2
9 − 3	8 − 4	7 − 5	9 − 5
9 − 9	5 − 3	8 − 2	6 − 6

Started: _____ Finished: _____ Total Time: _____ Completed: _____ Correct: _____

Name: _____   Date: _____

$$\begin{array}{r} 9 \\ -\ 5 \\ \hline \end{array} \qquad \begin{array}{r} 5 \\ -\ 5 \\ \hline \end{array} \qquad \begin{array}{r} 6 \\ -\ 0 \\ \hline \end{array} \qquad \begin{array}{r} 9 \\ -\ 4 \\ \hline \end{array} \qquad \begin{array}{r} 8 \\ -\ 4 \\ \hline \end{array}$$

$$\begin{array}{r} 7 \\ -\ 1 \\ \hline \end{array} \qquad \begin{array}{r} 5 \\ -\ 2 \\ \hline \end{array} \qquad \begin{array}{r} 8 \\ -\ 3 \\ \hline \end{array} \qquad \begin{array}{r} 10 \\ -\ 4 \\ \hline \end{array} \qquad \begin{array}{r} 6 \\ -\ 3 \\ \hline \end{array}$$

$$\begin{array}{r} 9 \\ -\ 1 \\ \hline \end{array} \qquad \begin{array}{r} 8 \\ -\ 2 \\ \hline \end{array} \qquad \begin{array}{r} 8 \\ -\ 0 \\ \hline \end{array} \qquad \begin{array}{r} 7 \\ -\ 4 \\ \hline \end{array} \qquad \begin{array}{r} 6 \\ -\ 5 \\ \hline \end{array}$$

$$\begin{array}{r} 5 \\ -\ 4 \\ \hline \end{array} \qquad \begin{array}{r} 3 \\ -\ 3 \\ \hline \end{array} \qquad \begin{array}{r} 6 \\ -\ 4 \\ \hline \end{array} \qquad \begin{array}{r} 10 \\ -\ 0 \\ \hline \end{array} \qquad \begin{array}{r} 4 \\ -\ 2 \\ \hline \end{array}$$

$$\begin{array}{r} 10 \\ -\ 6 \\ \hline \end{array} \qquad \begin{array}{r} 9 \\ -\ 3 \\ \hline \end{array} \qquad \begin{array}{r} 8 \\ -\ 8 \\ \hline \end{array} \qquad \begin{array}{r} 9 \\ -\ 6 \\ \hline \end{array} \qquad \begin{array}{r} 5 \\ -\ 3 \\ \hline \end{array}$$

$$\begin{array}{r} 9 \\ -\ 9 \\ \hline \end{array} \qquad \begin{array}{r} 7 \\ -\ 3 \\ \hline \end{array} \qquad \begin{array}{r} 3 \\ -\ 2 \\ \hline \end{array} \qquad \begin{array}{r} 4 \\ -\ 3 \\ \hline \end{array} \qquad \begin{array}{r} 8 \\ -\ 7 \\ \hline \end{array}$$

Started: Finished: Total Time: Completed: Correct:

Name: _____　　　　Date: _____

5 − 5	1 − 0	9 − 7	9 − 9	10 − 6
8 − 7	9 − 2	7 − 1	5 − 3	3 − 2
7 − 6	2 − 2	3 − 1	6 − 3	8 − 5
6 − 5	2 − 0	4 − 3	6 − 2	8 − 4
4 − 4	8 − 6	7 − 3	8 − 2	10 − 8
10 − 4	6 − 6	10 − 2	9 − 6	5 − 4

Started: _____　Finished: _____　Total Time: _____　Completed: _____　Correct: _____

Name: _____   Date: _____

5	9	10	8	6
− 2	− 0	− 4	− 6	− 2

9	10	7	5	10
− 1	− 5	− 4	− 0	− 8

7	8	5	9	7
− 5	− 7	− 4	− 3	− 7

6	2	7	10	9
− 5	− 0	− 6	− 9	− 5

6	7	8	9	10
− 4	− 3	− 8	− 4	− 0

6	7	8	9	9
− 3	− 2	− 5	− 8	− 6

Started: Finished: Total Time: Completed: Correct:

Name: _____   Date: _____

$$7 - 4 = $$ $$6 - 3 = $$ $$2 - 2 = $$ $$3 - 1 = $$ $$6 - 5 = $$

$$8 - 4 = $$ $$7 - 2 = $$ $$6 - 6 = $$ $$10 - 5 = $$ $$9 - 5 = $$

$$6 - 4 = $$ $$10 - 0 = $$ $$7 - 7 = $$ $$8 - 1 = $$ $$7 - 5 = $$

$$8 - 6 = $$ $$10 - 9 = $$ $$9 - 6 = $$ $$3 - 2 = $$ $$10 - 6 = $$

$$3 - 0 = $$ $$9 - 4 = $$ $$5 - 3 = $$ $$6 - 2 = $$ $$9 - 9 = $$

$$8 - 5 = $$ $$7 - 3 = $$ $$8 - 2 = $$ $$4 - 2 = $$ $$2 - 0 = $$

Started: Finished: Total Time: Completed: Correct:

Name: _____   Date: _____

18 − 9	17 − 8	16 − 9	14 − 6
16 − 7	15 − 9	13 − 6	14 − 7
13 − 4	12 − 8	11 − 7	12 − 6
15 − 6	11 − 9	16 − 8	13 − 7
11 − 4	15 − 8	14 − 5	14 − 8

Started: _____   Finished: _____   Total Time: _____   Completed: _____   Correct: _____

Name: _____

Date: _____

$$\begin{array}{r} 16 \\ -\ 9 \\ \hline \end{array} \qquad \begin{array}{r} 15 \\ -\ 8 \\ \hline \end{array} \qquad \begin{array}{r} 13 \\ -\ 9 \\ \hline \end{array} \qquad \begin{array}{r} 14 \\ -\ 7 \\ \hline \end{array}$$

$$\begin{array}{r} 17 \\ -\ 9 \\ \hline \end{array} \qquad \begin{array}{r} 17 \\ -\ 8 \\ \hline \end{array} \qquad \begin{array}{r} 18 \\ -\ 9 \\ \hline \end{array} \qquad \begin{array}{r} 14 \\ -\ 8 \\ \hline \end{array}$$

$$\begin{array}{r} 14 \\ -\ 9 \\ \hline \end{array} \qquad \begin{array}{r} 15 \\ -\ 6 \\ \hline \end{array} \qquad \begin{array}{r} 13 \\ -\ 5 \\ \hline \end{array} \qquad \begin{array}{r} 14 \\ -\ 6 \\ \hline \end{array}$$

$$\begin{array}{r} 11 \\ -\ 9 \\ \hline \end{array} \qquad \begin{array}{r} 12 \\ -\ 3 \\ \hline \end{array} \qquad \begin{array}{r} 14 \\ -\ 5 \\ \hline \end{array} \qquad \begin{array}{r} 16 \\ -\ 7 \\ \hline \end{array}$$

$$\begin{array}{r} 16 \\ -\ 8 \\ \hline \end{array} \qquad \begin{array}{r} 12 \\ -\ 5 \\ \hline \end{array} \qquad \begin{array}{r} 12 \\ -\ 6 \\ \hline \end{array} \qquad \begin{array}{r} 13 \\ -\ 7 \\ \hline \end{array}$$

Started: Finished: Total Time: Completed: Correct:

Name: _____ Date: _____

11 − 4	15 − 6	11 − 5	17 − 9
14 − 5	17 − 8	18 − 9	14 − 6
16 − 8	15 − 9	13 − 7	14 − 7
13 − 9	12 − 9	11 − 6	11 − 9
15 − 7	16 − 9	12 − 7	16 − 7

Started: _____ Finished: _____ Total Time: _____ Completed: _____ Correct: _____

Name: _____

Date: _____

$$\begin{array}{r} 18 \\ -\ 9 \\ \hline \end{array}$$
$$\begin{array}{r} 16 \\ -\ 7 \\ \hline \end{array}$$
$$\begin{array}{r} 14 \\ -\ 9 \\ \hline \end{array}$$
$$\begin{array}{r} 11 \\ -\ 2 \\ \hline \end{array}$$

$$\begin{array}{r} 12 \\ -\ 7 \\ \hline \end{array}$$
$$\begin{array}{r} 15 \\ -\ 8 \\ \hline \end{array}$$
$$\begin{array}{r} 13 \\ -\ 9 \\ \hline \end{array}$$
$$\begin{array}{r} 17 \\ -\ 8 \\ \hline \end{array}$$

$$\begin{array}{r} 14 \\ -\ 6 \\ \hline \end{array}$$
$$\begin{array}{r} 13 \\ -\ 6 \\ \hline \end{array}$$
$$\begin{array}{r} 11 \\ -\ 7 \\ \hline \end{array}$$
$$\begin{array}{r} 11 \\ -\ 9 \\ \hline \end{array}$$

$$\begin{array}{r} 12 \\ -\ 4 \\ \hline \end{array}$$
$$\begin{array}{r} 12 \\ -\ 9 \\ \hline \end{array}$$
$$\begin{array}{r} 14 \\ -\ 8 \\ \hline \end{array}$$
$$\begin{array}{r} 13 \\ -\ 7 \\ \hline \end{array}$$

$$\begin{array}{r} 11 \\ -\ 4 \\ \hline \end{array}$$
$$\begin{array}{r} 16 \\ -\ 8 \\ \hline \end{array}$$
$$\begin{array}{r} 11 \\ -\ 5 \\ \hline \end{array}$$
$$\begin{array}{r} 15 \\ -\ 9 \\ \hline \end{array}$$

Started: _____   Finished: _____   Total Time: _____   Completed: _____   Correct: _____

Name: _____   Date: _____

$$
\begin{array}{r} 16 \\ -\ 7 \\ \hline \end{array}
\qquad
\begin{array}{r} 14 \\ -\ 6 \\ \hline \end{array}
\qquad
\begin{array}{r} 12 \\ -\ 5 \\ \hline \end{array}
\qquad
\begin{array}{r} 13 \\ -\ 7 \\ \hline \end{array}
\qquad
\begin{array}{r} 15 \\ -\ 9 \\ \hline \end{array}
$$

$$
\begin{array}{r} 11 \\ -\ 6 \\ \hline \end{array}
\qquad
\begin{array}{r} 17 \\ -\ 9 \\ \hline \end{array}
\qquad
\begin{array}{r} 13 \\ -\ 9 \\ \hline \end{array}
\qquad
\begin{array}{r} 15 \\ -\ 8 \\ \hline \end{array}
\qquad
\begin{array}{r} 13 \\ -\ 8 \\ \hline \end{array}
$$

$$
\begin{array}{r} 15 \\ -\ 7 \\ \hline \end{array}
\qquad
\begin{array}{r} 14 \\ -\ 8 \\ \hline \end{array}
\qquad
\begin{array}{r} 13 \\ -\ 5 \\ \hline \end{array}
\qquad
\begin{array}{r} 12 \\ -\ 7 \\ \hline \end{array}
\qquad
\begin{array}{r} 11 \\ -\ 5 \\ \hline \end{array}
$$

$$
\begin{array}{r} 12 \\ -\ 4 \\ \hline \end{array}
\qquad
\begin{array}{r} 13 \\ -\ 6 \\ \hline \end{array}
\qquad
\begin{array}{r} 14 \\ -\ 7 \\ \hline \end{array}
\qquad
\begin{array}{r} 14 \\ -\ 9 \\ \hline \end{array}
\qquad
\begin{array}{r} 12 \\ -\ 6 \\ \hline \end{array}
$$

$$
\begin{array}{r} 11 \\ -\ 4 \\ \hline \end{array}
\qquad
\begin{array}{r} 16 \\ -\ 9 \\ \hline \end{array}
\qquad
\begin{array}{r} 12 \\ -\ 8 \\ \hline \end{array}
\qquad
\begin{array}{r} 11 \\ -\ 7 \\ \hline \end{array}
\qquad
\begin{array}{r} 18 \\ -\ 9 \\ \hline \end{array}
$$

$$
\begin{array}{r} 16 \\ -\ 8 \\ \hline \end{array}
\qquad
\begin{array}{r} 13 \\ -\ 4 \\ \hline \end{array}
\qquad
\begin{array}{r} 12 \\ -\ 9 \\ \hline \end{array}
\qquad
\begin{array}{r} 15 \\ -\ 6 \\ \hline \end{array}
\qquad
\begin{array}{r} 14 \\ -\ 5 \\ \hline \end{array}
$$

Started: _____   Finished: _____   Total Time: _____   Completed: _____   Correct: _____

Name: _____   Date: _____

18 − 9	14 − 6	15 − 6	13 − 7	14 − 9
17 − 8	16 − 8	13 − 9	16 − 9	13 − 5
15 − 9	14 − 7	13 − 8	12 − 8	11 − 7
13 − 4	12 − 9	16 − 7	11 − 8	12 − 6
11 − 9	12 − 5	13 − 6	11 − 5	17 − 9
14 − 5	15 − 7	15 − 8	14 − 8	12 − 7

Started: Finished: Total Time: Completed: Correct:

Name: _____   Date: _____

15 − 7	14 − 6	13 − 6	12 − 7	11 − 9
18 − 9	16 − 9	15 − 9	13 − 8	14 − 7
12 − 5	11 − 3	13 − 5	17 − 8	14 − 8
15 − 8	14 − 5	13 − 4	12 − 8	11 − 4
17 − 9	12 − 4	15 − 6	14 − 9	11 − 6
13 − 7	12 − 6	16 − 7	11 − 7	12 − 9

Started: _____   Finished: _____   Total Time: _____   Completed: _____   Correct: _____

Name: _____   Date: _____

11 − 6	14 − 9	12 − 9	15 − 6	18 − 9
17 − 8	11 − 4	13 − 9	17 − 9	13 − 7
11 − 3	12 − 7	14 − 7	13 − 8	14 − 5
15 − 7	11 − 5	13 − 6	11 − 8	12 − 6
13 − 4	14 − 6	12 − 8	11 − 7	16 − 9
16 − 7	13 − 5	11 − 2	15 − 8	11 − 9

Started: _____   Finished: _____   Total Time: _____   Completed: _____   Correct: _____

Name: _____   Date: _____

$$\begin{array}{r} 12 \\ -\ 5 \\ \hline \end{array} \qquad \begin{array}{r} 8 \\ -\ 7 \\ \hline \end{array} \qquad \begin{array}{r} 11 \\ -\ 7 \\ \hline \end{array} \qquad \begin{array}{r} 12 \\ -\ 6 \\ \hline \end{array}$$

$$\begin{array}{r} 13 \\ -\ 5 \\ \hline \end{array} \qquad \begin{array}{r} 16 \\ -\ 8 \\ \hline \end{array} \qquad \begin{array}{r} 15 \\ -\ 6 \\ \hline \end{array} \qquad \begin{array}{r} 17 \\ -\ 9 \\ \hline \end{array}$$

$$\begin{array}{r} 5 \\ -\ 4 \\ \hline \end{array} \qquad \begin{array}{r} 13 \\ -\ 9 \\ \hline \end{array} \qquad \begin{array}{r} 16 \\ -\ 7 \\ \hline \end{array} \qquad \begin{array}{r} 9 \\ -\ 8 \\ \hline \end{array}$$

$$\begin{array}{r} 14 \\ -\ 9 \\ \hline \end{array} \qquad \begin{array}{r} 13 \\ -\ 4 \\ \hline \end{array} \qquad \begin{array}{r} 12 \\ -\ 9 \\ \hline \end{array} \qquad \begin{array}{r} 11 \\ -\ 8 \\ \hline \end{array}$$

$$\begin{array}{r} 15 \\ -\ 7 \\ \hline \end{array} \qquad \begin{array}{r} 12 \\ -\ 4 \\ \hline \end{array} \qquad \begin{array}{r} 8 \\ -\ 6 \\ \hline \end{array} \qquad \begin{array}{r} 17 \\ -\ 8 \\ \hline \end{array}$$

Started: _____   Finished: _____   Total Time: _____   Completed: _____   Correct: _____

Name: _____   Date: _____

$$14 - 6$$ $$3 - 3$$ $$15 - 9$$ $$18 - 9$$

$$11 - 5$$ $$12 - 6$$ $$16 - 8$$ $$7 - 0$$

$$7 - 6$$ $$17 - 8$$ $$13 - 8$$ $$11 - 7$$

$$8 - 6$$ $$14 - 7$$ $$8 - 5$$ $$12 - 4$$

$$16 - 7$$ $$15 - 6$$ $$16 - 9$$ $$9 - 4$$

Started: Finished: Total Time: Completed: Correct:

Name: _____   Date: _____

$$\begin{array}{r} 12 \\ -\ 5 \\ \hline \end{array} \qquad \begin{array}{r} 12 \\ -\ 6 \\ \hline \end{array} \qquad \begin{array}{r} 16 \\ -\ 8 \\ \hline \end{array} \qquad \begin{array}{r} 7 \\ -\ 0 \\ \hline \end{array}$$

$$\begin{array}{r} 13 \\ -\ 6 \\ \hline \end{array} \qquad \begin{array}{r} 9 \\ -\ 7 \\ \hline \end{array} \qquad \begin{array}{r} 18 \\ -\ 9 \\ \hline \end{array} \qquad \begin{array}{r} 13 \\ -\ 6 \\ \hline \end{array}$$

$$\begin{array}{r} 13 \\ -\ 5 \\ \hline \end{array} \qquad \begin{array}{r} 16 \\ -\ 9 \\ \hline \end{array} \qquad \begin{array}{r} 15 \\ -\ 6 \\ \hline \end{array} \qquad \begin{array}{r} 17 \\ -\ 9 \\ \hline \end{array}$$

$$\begin{array}{r} 11 \\ -\ 4 \\ \hline \end{array} \qquad \begin{array}{r} 15 \\ -\ 9 \\ \hline \end{array} \qquad \begin{array}{r} 4 \\ -\ 1 \\ \hline \end{array} \qquad \begin{array}{r} 13 \\ -\ 7 \\ \hline \end{array}$$

$$\begin{array}{r} 16 \\ -\ 7 \\ \hline \end{array} \qquad \begin{array}{r} 15 \\ -\ 8 \\ \hline \end{array} \qquad \begin{array}{r} 13 \\ -\ 8 \\ \hline \end{array} \qquad \begin{array}{r} 6 \\ -\ 0 \\ \hline \end{array}$$

Started: _____   Finished: _____   Total Time: _____   Completed: _____   Correct: _____

Name: _____   Date: _____

$$\begin{array}{r} 14 \\ -\ 5 \\ \hline \end{array} \qquad \begin{array}{r} 12 \\ -\ 6 \\ \hline \end{array} \qquad \begin{array}{r} 18 \\ -\ 9 \\ \hline \end{array} \qquad \begin{array}{r} 17 \\ -\ 8 \\ \hline \end{array}$$

$$\begin{array}{r} 8 \\ -\ 5 \\ \hline \end{array} \qquad \begin{array}{r} 13 \\ -\ 4 \\ \hline \end{array} \qquad \begin{array}{r} 6 \\ -\ 5 \\ \hline \end{array} \qquad \begin{array}{r} 16 \\ -\ 8 \\ \hline \end{array}$$

$$\begin{array}{r} 12 \\ -\ 7 \\ \hline \end{array} \qquad \begin{array}{r} 15 \\ -\ 7 \\ \hline \end{array} \qquad \begin{array}{r} 11 \\ -\ 7 \\ \hline \end{array} \qquad \begin{array}{r} 12 \\ -\ 4 \\ \hline \end{array}$$

$$\begin{array}{r} 13 \\ -\ 5 \\ \hline \end{array} \qquad \begin{array}{r} 6 \\ -\ 4 \\ \hline \end{array} \qquad \begin{array}{r} 15 \\ -\ 6 \\ \hline \end{array} \qquad \begin{array}{r} 17 \\ -\ 9 \\ \hline \end{array}$$

$$\begin{array}{r} 14 \\ -\ 9 \\ \hline \end{array} \qquad \begin{array}{r} 13 \\ -\ 8 \\ \hline \end{array} \qquad \begin{array}{r} 9 \\ -\ 9 \\ \hline \end{array} \qquad \begin{array}{r} 11 \\ -\ 8 \\ \hline \end{array}$$

Started: Finished: Total Time: Completed: Correct:

Name: _____   Date: _____

7	12	18	11	12
− 5	− 3	− 9	− 7	− 6

13	16	8	15	17
− 5	− 8	− 4	− 6	− 9

15	9	13	16	14
− 8	− 6	− 9	− 7	− 6

14	13	12	5	11
− 9	− 4	− 9	− 0	− 8

15	9	12	13	17
− 7	− 7	− 4	− 6	− 8

13	14	9	11	16
− 7	− 8	− 4	− 6	− 9

Started: _____   Finished: _____   Total Time: _____   Completed: _____   Correct: _____

Name: _____

Date: _____

$$\begin{array}{r} 9 \\ -\ 0 \\ \hline \end{array} \qquad \begin{array}{r} 12 \\ -\ 5 \\ \hline \end{array} \qquad \begin{array}{r} 18 \\ -\ 9 \\ \hline \end{array} \qquad \begin{array}{r} 11 \\ -\ 6 \\ \hline \end{array} \qquad \begin{array}{r} 12 \\ -\ 8 \\ \hline \end{array}$$

$$\begin{array}{r} 10 \\ -\ 5 \\ \hline \end{array} \qquad \begin{array}{r} 13 \\ -\ 8 \\ \hline \end{array} \qquad \begin{array}{r} 16 \\ -\ 7 \\ \hline \end{array} \qquad \begin{array}{r} 15 \\ -\ 9 \\ \hline \end{array} \qquad \begin{array}{r} 17 \\ -\ 9 \\ \hline \end{array}$$

$$\begin{array}{r} 8 \\ -\ 4 \\ \hline \end{array} \qquad \begin{array}{r} 15 \\ -\ 8 \\ \hline \end{array} \qquad \begin{array}{r} 13 \\ -\ 7 \\ \hline \end{array} \qquad \begin{array}{r} 16 \\ -\ 8 \\ \hline \end{array} \qquad \begin{array}{r} 9 \\ -\ 8 \\ \hline \end{array}$$

$$\begin{array}{r} 12 \\ -\ 6 \\ \hline \end{array} \qquad \begin{array}{r} 8 \\ -\ 7 \\ \hline \end{array} \qquad \begin{array}{r} 14 \\ -\ 5 \\ \hline \end{array} \qquad \begin{array}{r} 8 \\ -\ 6 \\ \hline \end{array} \qquad \begin{array}{r} 12 \\ -\ 7 \\ \hline \end{array}$$

$$\begin{array}{r} 16 \\ -\ 9 \\ \hline \end{array} \qquad \begin{array}{r} 14 \\ -\ 7 \\ \hline \end{array} \qquad \begin{array}{r} 9 \\ -\ 6 \\ \hline \end{array} \qquad \begin{array}{r} 12 \\ -\ 9 \\ \hline \end{array} \qquad \begin{array}{r} 11 \\ -\ 7 \\ \hline \end{array}$$

$$\begin{array}{r} 7 \\ -\ 7 \\ \hline \end{array} \qquad \begin{array}{r} 15 \\ -\ 7 \\ \hline \end{array} \qquad \begin{array}{r} 10 \\ -\ 6 \\ \hline \end{array} \qquad \begin{array}{r} 14 \\ -\ 8 \\ \hline \end{array} \qquad \begin{array}{r} 7 \\ -\ 4 \\ \hline \end{array}$$

Started: _____   Finished: _____   Total Time: _____   Completed: _____   Correct: _____

Name: _____ Date: _____

$\begin{array}{r} 8 \\ -6 \\ \hline \end{array}$	$\begin{array}{r} 14 \\ -7 \\ \hline \end{array}$	$\begin{array}{r} 13 \\ -9 \\ \hline \end{array}$	$\begin{array}{r} 11 \\ -6 \\ \hline \end{array}$	$\begin{array}{r} 18 \\ -9 \\ \hline \end{array}$
$\begin{array}{r} 11 \\ -4 \\ \hline \end{array}$	$\begin{array}{r} 12 \\ -5 \\ \hline \end{array}$	$\begin{array}{r} 16 \\ -9 \\ \hline \end{array}$	$\begin{array}{r} 17 \\ -8 \\ \hline \end{array}$	$\begin{array}{r} 5 \\ -2 \\ \hline \end{array}$
$\begin{array}{r} 16 \\ -8 \\ \hline \end{array}$	$\begin{array}{r} 13 \\ -4 \\ \hline \end{array}$	$\begin{array}{r} 8 \\ -8 \\ \hline \end{array}$	$\begin{array}{r} 13 \\ -7 \\ \hline \end{array}$	$\begin{array}{r} 10 \\ -9 \\ \hline \end{array}$
$\begin{array}{r} 13 \\ -6 \\ \hline \end{array}$	$\begin{array}{r} 14 \\ -6 \\ \hline \end{array}$	$\begin{array}{r} 12 \\ -7 \\ \hline \end{array}$	$\begin{array}{r} 12 \\ -9 \\ \hline \end{array}$	$\begin{array}{r} 9 \\ -6 \\ \hline \end{array}$
$\begin{array}{r} 10 \\ -8 \\ \hline \end{array}$	$\begin{array}{r} 16 \\ -7 \\ \hline \end{array}$	$\begin{array}{r} 15 \\ -8 \\ \hline \end{array}$	$\begin{array}{r} 12 \\ -4 \\ \hline \end{array}$	$\begin{array}{r} 14 \\ -8 \\ \hline \end{array}$
$\begin{array}{r} 13 \\ -5 \\ \hline \end{array}$	$\begin{array}{r} 15 \\ -7 \\ \hline \end{array}$	$\begin{array}{r} 8 \\ -4 \\ \hline \end{array}$	$\begin{array}{r} 15 \\ -6 \\ \hline \end{array}$	$\begin{array}{r} 17 \\ -9 \\ \hline \end{array}$

Started: _____ Finished: _____ Total Time: _____ Completed: _____ Correct: _____

Name: _____   Date: _____

14 − 5	12 − 6	9 − 8	6 − 0	17 − 8
11 − 6	10 − 6	14 − 9	8 − 6	12 − 9
7 − 5	13 − 8	16 − 9	15 − 8	18 − 9
11 − 4	15 − 9	4 − 1	13 − 7	13 − 9
16 − 7	14 − 8	15 − 6	7 − 4	16 − 8
12 − 4	9 − 6	13 − 5	10 − 7	12 − 8

Started: Finished: Total Time: Completed: Correct:

Name: _____ Date: _____

7 − 4	14 − 6	12 − 4	8 − 3	10 − 3
8 − 6	5 − 4	18 − 9	13 − 7	9 − 6
7 − 2	15 − 6	13 − 8	16 − 8	11 − 8
9 − 7	12 − 5	14 − 7	11 − 6	12 − 9
8 − 5	13 − 5	16 − 7	15 − 9	14 − 9
9 − 9	14 − 5	13 − 9	12 − 8	11 − 4

Started: _____   Finished: _____   Total Time: _____   Completed: _____   Correct: _____

Name: _____   Date: _____

$$\begin{array}{r} 5 \\ -4 \\ \hline \end{array} \qquad \begin{array}{r} 14 \\ -6 \\ \hline \end{array} \qquad \begin{array}{r} 13 \\ -4 \\ \hline \end{array} \qquad \begin{array}{r} 12 \\ -7 \\ \hline \end{array} \qquad \begin{array}{r} 11 \\ -3 \\ \hline \end{array}$$

$$\begin{array}{r} 7 \\ -7 \\ \hline \end{array} \qquad \begin{array}{r} 14 \\ -9 \\ \hline \end{array} \qquad \begin{array}{r} 12 \\ -6 \\ \hline \end{array} \qquad \begin{array}{r} 8 \\ -6 \\ \hline \end{array} \qquad \begin{array}{r} 7 \\ -2 \\ \hline \end{array}$$

$$\begin{array}{r} 11 \\ -5 \\ \hline \end{array} \qquad \begin{array}{r} 2 \\ -2 \\ \hline \end{array} \qquad \begin{array}{r} 13 \\ -6 \\ \hline \end{array} \qquad \begin{array}{r} 14 \\ -8 \\ \hline \end{array} \qquad \begin{array}{r} 15 \\ -9 \\ \hline \end{array}$$

$$\begin{array}{r} 9 \\ -4 \\ \hline \end{array} \qquad \begin{array}{r} 18 \\ -9 \\ \hline \end{array} \qquad \begin{array}{r} 11 \\ -8 \\ \hline \end{array} \qquad \begin{array}{r} 15 \\ -7 \\ \hline \end{array} \qquad \begin{array}{r} 13 \\ -9 \\ \hline \end{array}$$

$$\begin{array}{r} 10 \\ -7 \\ \hline \end{array} \qquad \begin{array}{r} 12 \\ -9 \\ \hline \end{array} \qquad \begin{array}{r} 16 \\ -7 \\ \hline \end{array} \qquad \begin{array}{r} 11 \\ -6 \\ \hline \end{array} \qquad \begin{array}{r} 12 \\ -5 \\ \hline \end{array}$$

$$\begin{array}{r} 9 \\ -5 \\ \hline \end{array} \qquad \begin{array}{r} 17 \\ -8 \\ \hline \end{array} \qquad \begin{array}{r} 11 \\ -2 \\ \hline \end{array} \qquad \begin{array}{r} 16 \\ -9 \\ \hline \end{array} \qquad \begin{array}{r} 13 \\ -8 \\ \hline \end{array}$$

$$\begin{array}{r} 6 \\ -4 \\ \hline \end{array} \qquad \begin{array}{r} 12 \\ -4 \\ \hline \end{array} \qquad \begin{array}{r} 15 \\ -8 \\ \hline \end{array} \qquad \begin{array}{r} 11 \\ -7 \\ \hline \end{array} \qquad \begin{array}{r} 10 \\ -9 \\ \hline \end{array}$$

$$\begin{array}{r} 9 \\ -6 \\ \hline \end{array} \qquad \begin{array}{r} 12 \\ -8 \\ \hline \end{array} \qquad \begin{array}{r} 16 \\ -8 \\ \hline \end{array} \qquad \begin{array}{r} 11 \\ -9 \\ \hline \end{array} \qquad \begin{array}{r} 14 \\ -7 \\ \hline \end{array}$$

Started: _____   Finished: _____   Total Time: _____   Completed: _____   Correct: _____

Name: _____   Date: _____

10 − 9	18 − 9	9 − 6	12 − 6	8 − 0
8 − 5	13 − 8	16 − 7	15 − 9	14 − 9
14 − 5	10 − 8	4 − 3	7 − 0	8 − 3
13 − 9	9 − 3	10 − 2	17 − 9	6 − 4
13 − 5	9 − 7	14 − 6	13 − 6	6 − 0
10 − 5	12 − 8	13 − 7	15 − 7	12 − 7
14 − 8	10 − 7	3 − 3	17 − 8	11 − 5
11 − 9	10 − 3	9 − 2	13 − 4	8 − 4

Started: Finished: Total Time: Completed: Correct:

Name: _____   Date: _____

12 − 3	10 − 6	11 − 7	9 − 6	5 − 5
9 − 4	13 − 9	8 − 3	11 − 6	12 − 5
9 − 8	16 − 9	15 − 6	13 − 7	14 − 6
10 − 3	14 − 8	13 − 4	12 − 9	11 − 8
10 − 9	13 − 8	15 − 9	17 − 8	7 − 4
18 − 9	12 − 7	10 − 0	15 − 8	14 − 9
13 − 5	9 − 3	8 − 4	17 − 9	9 − 7
9 − 5	16 − 7	14 − 7	13 − 6	4 − 4

Started: _____ Finished: _____ Total Time: _____ Completed: _____ Correct: _____

Name: _____   Date: _____

12 − 6	10 − 9	13 − 6	8 − 4	14 − 5
11 − 5	10 − 1	4 − 3	17 − 8	8 − 3
9 − 6	15 − 7	17 − 8	8 − 6	6 − 6
3 − 2	17 − 9	11 − 8	5 − 3	13 − 9
12 − 4	16 − 8	11 − 2	9 − 9	13 − 8
9 − 7	16 − 9	15 − 6	13 − 7	14 − 6
7 − 6	13 − 5	12 − 7	11 − 6	12 − 8
14 − 9	9 − 4	15 − 8	8 − 7	16 − 7

Started: Finished: Total Time: Completed: Correct:

Name: _____   Date: _____

14 − 5	12 − 9	18 − 9	11 − 6	12 − 3
7 − 7	15 − 6	17 − 8	16 − 9	14 − 6
11 − 4	13 − 9	14 − 8	9 − 7	13 − 8
12 − 4	8 − 6	14 − 7	15 − 9	8 − 3
14 − 9	13 − 5	15 − 7	11 − 8	12 − 7
4 − 2	10 − 3	7 − 0	16 − 8	13 − 6
8 − 4	13 − 7	11 − 2	7 − 5	13 − 4
11 − 5	6 − 6	16 − 7	15 − 8	8 − 2

Started: Finished: Total Time: Completed: Correct:

Name: _____   Date: _____

17 − 8	14 − 7	12 − 8	18 − 9	7 − 3
8 − 4	16 − 8	11 − 7	9 − 9	13 − 8
7 − 6	10 − 4	13 − 4	10 − 7	8 − 8
9 − 4	7 − 4	15 − 9	16 − 7	12 − 9
12 − 7	12 − 6	8 − 0	11 − 4	7 − 7
6 − 5	14 − 8	17 − 9	15 − 6	13 − 6
9 − 7	12 − 5	5 − 4	11 − 6	12 − 3
7 − 5	13 − 7	6 − 3	15 − 7	14 − 6
11 − 5	14 − 5	13 − 9	12 − 4	9 − 3
9 − 5	15 − 8	11 − 8	16 − 9	13 − 5

Started: Finished: Total Time: Completed: Correct:

Name: _____   Date: _____

9 − 7	8 − 0	14 − 7	8 − 6	7 − 2
11 − 4	15 − 6	7 − 4	13 − 7	10 − 3
12 − 7	7 − 1	14 − 9	8 − 3	7 − 7
15 − 7	11 − 9	8 − 8	8 − 7	15 − 9
14 − 6	11 − 2	12 − 6	13 − 5	15 − 8
9 − 4	9 − 9	8 − 2	11 − 7	13 − 9
8 − 4	7 − 0	12 − 5	11 − 6	12 − 9
8 − 5	9 − 8	9 − 2	11 − 3	14 − 8
6 − 4	10 − 9	11 − 8	8 − 1	13 − 8
11 − 5	9 − 3	12 − 8	16 − 9	14 − 5

Started: _____   Finished: _____   Total Time: _____   Completed: _____   Correct: _____

Name: _____   Date: _____

16 − 8	13 − 7	9 − 6	15 − 8	18 − 9
11 − 7	10 − 9	15 − 7	8 − 6	13 − 5
12 − 5	8 − 8	13 − 6	16 − 9	14 − 6
12 − 4	10 − 7	14 − 9	17 − 8	8 − 3
10 − 5	17 − 9	9 − 2	12 − 6	8 − 4
12 − 7	10 − 6	9 − 7	14 − 8	12 − 3
9 − 4	15 − 6	8 − 2	13 − 4	6 − 5
8 − 0	13 − 8	14 − 7	16 − 7	12 − 8
11 − 5	12 − 9	9 − 3	11 − 9	8 − 5
14 − 5	15 − 9	9 − 5	13 − 9	7 − 4

Started: _____ Finished: _____ Total Time: _____ Completed: _____ Correct: _____

Name: _____   Date: _____

13 − 7	18 − 9	11 − 7	9 − 6	5 − 5
9 − 3	13 − 4	9 − 4	8 − 6	7 − 5
10 − 6	16 − 9	15 − 6	13 − 6	14 − 6
14 − 5	12 − 8	8 − 4	13 − 9	16 − 7
11 − 3	9 − 8	16 − 8	9 − 9	12 − 5
15 − 9	10 − 4	13 − 8	17 − 8	7 − 4
12 − 9	10 − 3	13 − 5	8 − 5	14 − 8
15 − 8	6 − 0	12 − 6	10 − 5	10 − 7
12 − 3	17 − 9	8 − 2	7 − 6	9 − 5
9 − 0	15 − 7	8 − 3	12 − 7	14 − 7

Started: _____   Finished: _____   Total Time: _____   Completed: _____   Correct: _____

Name: _____   Date: _____

17 − 8	14 − 9	10 − 8	13 − 7	18 − 9
7 − 6	10 − 7	13 − 6	8 − 4	14 − 6
7 − 3	11 − 8	10 − 4	14 − 7	15 − 6
15 − 9	11 − 3	8 − 0	6 − 4	9 − 6
9 − 4	15 − 8	11 − 6	9 − 7	10 − 6
13 − 8	8 − 8	11 − 2	17 − 9	16 − 8
6 − 0	16 − 9	15 − 7	13 − 9	14 − 8
7 − 4	13 − 5	12 − 7	9 − 5	12 − 6
14 − 5	9 − 9	13 − 4	8 − 3	16 − 7
8 − 7	12 − 8	6 − 2	10 − 9	10 − 5

Started: _____ Finished: _____ Total Time: _____ Completed: _____ Correct: _____

Name: _____   Date: _____

8 − 7	12 − 6	16 − 7	11 − 6	12 − 8
15 − 7	13 − 4	17 − 9	18 − 9	12 − 4
17 − 8	14 − 9	15 − 8	10 − 8	14 − 8
12 − 9	14 − 5	8 − 5	11 − 9	16 − 8
14 − 7	8 − 6	11 − 8	4 − 4	9 − 3
11 − 4	9 − 5	13 − 8	13 − 5	16 − 9
11 − 7	6 − 5	12 − 3	15 − 6	8 − 8
10 − 6	13 − 9	9 − 7	3 − 2	7 − 4
11 − 5	13 − 6	15 − 9	1 − 0	12 − 7
12 − 5	9 − 9	10 − 5	14 − 6	9 − 6

Started: _____   Finished: _____   Total Time: _____   Completed: _____   Correct: _____

Name: _____   Date: _____

$$\begin{array}{r} 1 \\ \times\,0 \\ \hline \end{array} \qquad \begin{array}{r} 2 \\ \times\,1 \\ \hline \end{array} \qquad \begin{array}{r} 3 \\ \times\,2 \\ \hline \end{array} \qquad \begin{array}{r} 2 \\ \times\,2 \\ \hline \end{array}$$

$$\begin{array}{r} 4 \\ \times\,2 \\ \hline \end{array} \qquad \begin{array}{r} 5 \\ \times\,2 \\ \hline \end{array} \qquad \begin{array}{r} 1 \\ \times\,1 \\ \hline \end{array} \qquad \begin{array}{r} 3 \\ \times\,1 \\ \hline \end{array}$$

$$\begin{array}{r} 4 \\ \times\,1 \\ \hline \end{array} \qquad \begin{array}{r} 6 \\ \times\,2 \\ \hline \end{array} \qquad \begin{array}{r} 5 \\ \times\,1 \\ \hline \end{array} \qquad \begin{array}{r} 8 \\ \times\,1 \\ \hline \end{array}$$

$$\begin{array}{r} 7 \\ \times\,1 \\ \hline \end{array} \qquad \begin{array}{r} 8 \\ \times\,2 \\ \hline \end{array} \qquad \begin{array}{r} 3 \\ \times\,0 \\ \hline \end{array} \qquad \begin{array}{r} 7 \\ \times\,2 \\ \hline \end{array}$$

$$\begin{array}{r} 6 \\ \times\,1 \\ \hline \end{array} \qquad \begin{array}{r} 9 \\ \times\,2 \\ \hline \end{array} \qquad \begin{array}{r} 7 \\ \times\,0 \\ \hline \end{array} \qquad \begin{array}{r} 9 \\ \times\,1 \\ \hline \end{array}$$

Started: _____   Finished: _____   Total Time: _____   Completed: _____   Correct: _____

Name: _____   Date: _____

$$
\begin{array}{r} 7 \\ \times\,0 \\ \hline \end{array}
\qquad
\begin{array}{r} 8 \\ \times\,1 \\ \hline \end{array}
\qquad
\begin{array}{r} 3 \\ \times\,2 \\ \hline \end{array}
\qquad
\begin{array}{r} 7 \\ \times\,3 \\ \hline \end{array}
$$

$$
\begin{array}{r} 6 \\ \times\,3 \\ \hline \end{array}
\qquad
\begin{array}{r} 9 \\ \times\,2 \\ \hline \end{array}
\qquad
\begin{array}{r} 7 \\ \times\,1 \\ \hline \end{array}
\qquad
\begin{array}{r} 9 \\ \times\,0 \\ \hline \end{array}
$$

$$
\begin{array}{r} 5 \\ \times\,1 \\ \hline \end{array}
\qquad
\begin{array}{r} 4 \\ \times\,3 \\ \hline \end{array}
\qquad
\begin{array}{r} 6 \\ \times\,0 \\ \hline \end{array}
\qquad
\begin{array}{r} 5 \\ \times\,3 \\ \hline \end{array}
$$

$$
\begin{array}{r} 2 \\ \times\,3 \\ \hline \end{array}
\qquad
\begin{array}{r} 8 \\ \times\,2 \\ \hline \end{array}
\qquad
\begin{array}{r} 4 \\ \times\,1 \\ \hline \end{array}
\qquad
\begin{array}{r} 8 \\ \times\,3 \\ \hline \end{array}
$$

$$
\begin{array}{r} 2 \\ \times\,2 \\ \hline \end{array}
\qquad
\begin{array}{r} 3 \\ \times\,3 \\ \hline \end{array}
\qquad
\begin{array}{r} 9 \\ \times\,3 \\ \hline \end{array}
\qquad
\begin{array}{r} 4 \\ \times\,0 \\ \hline \end{array}
$$

Started: Finished: Total Time: Completed: Correct:

Name: _____   Date: _____

$$\begin{array}{r} 1 \\ \times\,0 \\ \hline \end{array} \qquad \begin{array}{r} 1 \\ \times\,1 \\ \hline \end{array} \qquad \begin{array}{r} 9 \\ \times\,3 \\ \hline \end{array} \qquad \begin{array}{r} 3 \\ \times\,2 \\ \hline \end{array} \qquad \begin{array}{r} 2 \\ \times\,1 \\ \hline \end{array}$$

$$\begin{array}{r} 4 \\ \times\,0 \\ \hline \end{array} \qquad \begin{array}{r} 5 \\ \times\,2 \\ \hline \end{array} \qquad \begin{array}{r} 5 \\ \times\,3 \\ \hline \end{array} \qquad \begin{array}{r} 3 \\ \times\,1 \\ \hline \end{array} \qquad \begin{array}{r} 8 \\ \times\,1 \\ \hline \end{array}$$

$$\begin{array}{r} 2 \\ \times\,0 \\ \hline \end{array} \qquad \begin{array}{r} 6 \\ \times\,1 \\ \hline \end{array} \qquad \begin{array}{r} 7 \\ \times\,2 \\ \hline \end{array} \qquad \begin{array}{r} 7 \\ \times\,3 \\ \hline \end{array} \qquad \begin{array}{r} 9 \\ \times\,1 \\ \hline \end{array}$$

$$\begin{array}{r} 4 \\ \times\,1 \\ \hline \end{array} \qquad \begin{array}{r} 5 \\ \times\,1 \\ \hline \end{array} \qquad \begin{array}{r} 4 \\ \times\,2 \\ \hline \end{array} \qquad \begin{array}{r} 7 \\ \times\,0 \\ \hline \end{array} \qquad \begin{array}{r} 6 \\ \times\,2 \\ \hline \end{array}$$

$$\begin{array}{r} 4 \\ \times\,3 \\ \hline \end{array} \qquad \begin{array}{r} 9 \\ \times\,0 \\ \hline \end{array} \qquad \begin{array}{r} 8 \\ \times\,2 \\ \hline \end{array} \qquad \begin{array}{r} 9 \\ \times\,2 \\ \hline \end{array} \qquad \begin{array}{r} 3 \\ \times\,0 \\ \hline \end{array}$$

$$\begin{array}{r} 6 \\ \times\,0 \\ \hline \end{array} \qquad \begin{array}{r} 7 \\ \times\,1 \\ \hline \end{array} \qquad \begin{array}{r} 2 \\ \times\,2 \\ \hline \end{array} \qquad \begin{array}{r} 1 \\ \times\,2 \\ \hline \end{array} \qquad \begin{array}{r} 8 \\ \times\,3 \\ \hline \end{array}$$

Started: _____ Finished: _____ Total Time: _____ Completed: _____ Correct: _____

Name: _____   Date: _____

$$
\begin{array}{r} 1 \\ \times\,2 \\ \hline \end{array}
\qquad
\begin{array}{r} 2 \\ \times\,1 \\ \hline \end{array}
\qquad
\begin{array}{r} 5 \\ \times\,2 \\ \hline \end{array}
\qquad
\begin{array}{r} 6 \\ \times\,0 \\ \hline \end{array}
\qquad
\begin{array}{r} 4 \\ \times\,1 \\ \hline \end{array}
$$

$$
\begin{array}{r} 3 \\ \times\,2 \\ \hline \end{array}
\qquad
\begin{array}{r} 7 \\ \times\,0 \\ \hline \end{array}
\qquad
\begin{array}{r} 7 \\ \times\,1 \\ \hline \end{array}
\qquad
\begin{array}{r} 8 \\ \times\,2 \\ \hline \end{array}
\qquad
\begin{array}{r} 3 \\ \times\,3 \\ \hline \end{array}
$$

$$
\begin{array}{r} 7 \\ \times\,2 \\ \hline \end{array}
\qquad
\begin{array}{r} 9 \\ \times\,3 \\ \hline \end{array}
\qquad
\begin{array}{r} 6 \\ \times\,2 \\ \hline \end{array}
\qquad
\begin{array}{r} 9 \\ \times\,1 \\ \hline \end{array}
\qquad
\begin{array}{r} 8 \\ \times\,0 \\ \hline \end{array}
$$

$$
\begin{array}{r} 1 \\ \times\,3 \\ \hline \end{array}
\qquad
\begin{array}{r} 5 \\ \times\,1 \\ \hline \end{array}
\qquad
\begin{array}{r} 5 \\ \times\,3 \\ \hline \end{array}
\qquad
\begin{array}{r} 4 \\ \times\,0 \\ \hline \end{array}
\qquad
\begin{array}{r} 6 \\ \times\,3 \\ \hline \end{array}
$$

$$
\begin{array}{r} 6 \\ \times\,1 \\ \hline \end{array}
\qquad
\begin{array}{r} 8 \\ \times\,3 \\ \hline \end{array}
\qquad
\begin{array}{r} 2 \\ \times\,2 \\ \hline \end{array}
\qquad
\begin{array}{r} 8 \\ \times\,1 \\ \hline \end{array}
\qquad
\begin{array}{r} 4 \\ \times\,3 \\ \hline \end{array}
$$

$$
\begin{array}{r} 5 \\ \times\,0 \\ \hline \end{array}
\qquad
\begin{array}{r} 4 \\ \times\,2 \\ \hline \end{array}
\qquad
\begin{array}{r} 2 \\ \times\,3 \\ \hline \end{array}
\qquad
\begin{array}{r} 7 \\ \times\,3 \\ \hline \end{array}
\qquad
\begin{array}{r} 9 \\ \times\,0 \\ \hline \end{array}
$$

Started: _____   Finished: _____   Total Time: _____   Completed: _____   Correct: _____

Name: _____   Date: _____

$$
\begin{array}{r} 5 \\ \times 4 \\ \hline \end{array}
\qquad
\begin{array}{r} 4 \\ \times 3 \\ \hline \end{array}
\qquad
\begin{array}{r} 6 \\ \times 2 \\ \hline \end{array}
\qquad
\begin{array}{r} 5 \\ \times 1 \\ \hline \end{array}
$$

$$
\begin{array}{r} 7 \\ \times 1 \\ \hline \end{array}
\qquad
\begin{array}{r} 8 \\ \times 2 \\ \hline \end{array}
\qquad
\begin{array}{r} 3 \\ \times 3 \\ \hline \end{array}
\qquad
\begin{array}{r} 7 \\ \times 4 \\ \hline \end{array}
$$

$$
\begin{array}{r} 6 \\ \times 4 \\ \hline \end{array}
\qquad
\begin{array}{r} 9 \\ \times 3 \\ \hline \end{array}
\qquad
\begin{array}{r} 7 \\ \times 2 \\ \hline \end{array}
\qquad
\begin{array}{r} 9 \\ \times 1 \\ \hline \end{array}
$$

$$
\begin{array}{r} 5 \\ \times 0 \\ \hline \end{array}
\qquad
\begin{array}{r} 4 \\ \times 4 \\ \hline \end{array}
\qquad
\begin{array}{r} 9 \\ \times 4 \\ \hline \end{array}
\qquad
\begin{array}{r} 6 \\ \times 1 \\ \hline \end{array}
$$

$$
\begin{array}{r} 6 \\ \times 3 \\ \hline \end{array}
\qquad
\begin{array}{r} 4 \\ \times 2 \\ \hline \end{array}
\qquad
\begin{array}{r} 8 \\ \times 4 \\ \hline \end{array}
\qquad
\begin{array}{r} 7 \\ \times 3 \\ \hline \end{array}
$$

Started: _____   Finished: _____   Total Time: _____   Completed: _____   Correct: _____

Name: _____   Date: _____

5 × 3	5 × 4	4 × 2	6 × 1	5 × 2
3 × 0	7 × 2	8 × 3	3 × 4	7 × 3
7 × 4	6 × 3	9 × 2	7 × 1	9 × 1
5 × 1	8 × 1	4 × 0	8 × 4	8 × 0
4 × 3	3 × 2	4 × 4	9 × 3	6 × 2
6 × 4	8 × 2	3 × 1	3 × 3	7 × 0

Started: _____   Finished: _____   Total Time: _____   Completed: _____   Correct: _____

Name: _____   Date: _____

$$\begin{array}{r} 5 \\ \times\,2 \\ \hline \end{array} \qquad \begin{array}{r} 7 \\ \times\,3 \\ \hline \end{array} \qquad \begin{array}{r} 8 \\ \times\,4 \\ \hline \end{array} \qquad \begin{array}{r} 4 \\ \times\,2 \\ \hline \end{array}$$

$$\begin{array}{r} 4 \\ \times\,4 \\ \hline \end{array} \qquad \begin{array}{r} 5 \\ \times\,5 \\ \hline \end{array} \qquad \begin{array}{r} 5 \\ \times\,3 \\ \hline \end{array} \qquad \begin{array}{r} 3 \\ \times\,1 \\ \hline \end{array}$$

$$\begin{array}{r} 7 \\ \times\,5 \\ \hline \end{array} \qquad \begin{array}{r} 5 \\ \times\,4 \\ \hline \end{array} \qquad \begin{array}{r} 8 \\ \times\,3 \\ \hline \end{array} \qquad \begin{array}{r} 9 \\ \times\,2 \\ \hline \end{array}$$

$$\begin{array}{r} 9 \\ \times\,4 \\ \hline \end{array} \qquad \begin{array}{r} 6 \\ \times\,5 \\ \hline \end{array} \qquad \begin{array}{r} 8 \\ \times\,2 \\ \hline \end{array} \qquad \begin{array}{r} 8 \\ \times\,1 \\ \hline \end{array}$$

$$\begin{array}{r} 7 \\ \times\,4 \\ \hline \end{array} \qquad \begin{array}{r} 8 \\ \times\,5 \\ \hline \end{array} \qquad \begin{array}{r} 7 \\ \times\,2 \\ \hline \end{array} \qquad \begin{array}{r} 5 \\ \times\,0 \\ \hline \end{array}$$

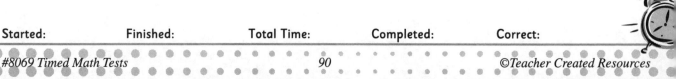

Started: _____ Finished: _____ Total Time: _____ Completed: _____ Correct: _____

Name: _____   Date: _____

$$\begin{array}{r} 3 \\ \times\,4 \\ \hline \end{array} \qquad \begin{array}{r} 7 \\ \times\,1 \\ \hline \end{array} \qquad \begin{array}{r} 8 \\ \times\,2 \\ \hline \end{array} \qquad \begin{array}{r} 3 \\ \times\,3 \\ \hline \end{array} \qquad \begin{array}{r} 7 \\ \times\,5 \\ \hline \end{array}$$

$$\begin{array}{r} 2 \\ \times\,5 \\ \hline \end{array} \qquad \begin{array}{r} 6 \\ \times\,2 \\ \hline \end{array} \qquad \begin{array}{r} 9 \\ \times\,1 \\ \hline \end{array} \qquad \begin{array}{r} 7 \\ \times\,0 \\ \hline \end{array} \qquad \begin{array}{r} 9 \\ \times\,3 \\ \hline \end{array}$$

$$\begin{array}{r} 7 \\ \times\,4 \\ \hline \end{array} \qquad \begin{array}{r} 5 \\ \times\,3 \\ \hline \end{array} \qquad \begin{array}{r} 4 \\ \times\,1 \\ \hline \end{array} \qquad \begin{array}{r} 6 \\ \times\,3 \\ \hline \end{array} \qquad \begin{array}{r} 5 \\ \times\,4 \\ \hline \end{array}$$

$$\begin{array}{r} 8 \\ \times\,3 \\ \hline \end{array} \qquad \begin{array}{r} 2 \\ \times\,2 \\ \hline \end{array} \qquad \begin{array}{r} 6 \\ \times\,1 \\ \hline \end{array} \qquad \begin{array}{r} 4 \\ \times\,4 \\ \hline \end{array} \qquad \begin{array}{r} 8 \\ \times\,5 \\ \hline \end{array}$$

$$\begin{array}{r} 6 \\ \times\,5 \\ \hline \end{array} \qquad \begin{array}{r} 2 \\ \times\,3 \\ \hline \end{array} \qquad \begin{array}{r} 6 \\ \times\,4 \\ \hline \end{array} \qquad \begin{array}{r} 9 \\ \times\,0 \\ \hline \end{array} \qquad \begin{array}{r} 5 \\ \times\,5 \\ \hline \end{array}$$

$$\begin{array}{r} 7 \\ \times\,3 \\ \hline \end{array} \qquad \begin{array}{r} 9 \\ \times\,5 \\ \hline \end{array} \qquad \begin{array}{r} 8 \\ \times\,1 \\ \hline \end{array} \qquad \begin{array}{r} 1 \\ \times\,5 \\ \hline \end{array} \qquad \begin{array}{r} 4 \\ \times\,2 \\ \hline \end{array}$$

Started: _____   Finished: _____   Total Time: _____   Completed: _____   Correct: _____

Name: _____   Date: _____

$$\begin{array}{r} 2 \\ \times\,6 \\ \hline \end{array} \qquad \begin{array}{r} 4 \\ \times\,6 \\ \hline \end{array} \qquad \begin{array}{r} 6 \\ \times\,6 \\ \hline \end{array} \qquad \begin{array}{r} 8 \\ \times\,6 \\ \hline \end{array}$$

$$\begin{array}{r} 1 \\ \times\,7 \\ \hline \end{array} \qquad \begin{array}{r} 3 \\ \times\,7 \\ \hline \end{array} \qquad \begin{array}{r} 5 \\ \times\,7 \\ \hline \end{array} \qquad \begin{array}{r} 7 \\ \times\,7 \\ \hline \end{array}$$

$$\begin{array}{r} 1 \\ \times\,6 \\ \hline \end{array} \qquad \begin{array}{r} 3 \\ \times\,6 \\ \hline \end{array} \qquad \begin{array}{r} 5 \\ \times\,6 \\ \hline \end{array} \qquad \begin{array}{r} 7 \\ \times\,6 \\ \hline \end{array}$$

$$\begin{array}{r} 2 \\ \times\,7 \\ \hline \end{array} \qquad \begin{array}{r} 4 \\ \times\,7 \\ \hline \end{array} \qquad \begin{array}{r} 6 \\ \times\,7 \\ \hline \end{array} \qquad \begin{array}{r} 8 \\ \times\,7 \\ \hline \end{array}$$

$$\begin{array}{r} 0 \\ \times\,6 \\ \hline \end{array} \qquad \begin{array}{r} 9 \\ \times\,6 \\ \hline \end{array} \qquad \begin{array}{r} 0 \\ \times\,7 \\ \hline \end{array} \qquad \begin{array}{r} 9 \\ \times\,7 \\ \hline \end{array}$$

Started: _____   Finished: _____   Total Time: _____   Completed: _____   Correct: _____

Name: _____   Date: _____

$$\begin{array}{r} 8 \\ \times\,6 \\ \hline \end{array} \qquad \begin{array}{r} 9 \\ \times\,8 \\ \hline \end{array} \qquad \begin{array}{r} 6 \\ \times\,6 \\ \hline \end{array} \qquad \begin{array}{r} 2 \\ \times\,6 \\ \hline \end{array}$$

$$\begin{array}{r} 5 \\ \times\,7 \\ \hline \end{array} \qquad \begin{array}{r} 3 \\ \times\,7 \\ \hline \end{array} \qquad \begin{array}{r} 7 \\ \times\,7 \\ \hline \end{array} \qquad \begin{array}{r} 6 \\ \times\,7 \\ \hline \end{array}$$

$$\begin{array}{r} 2 \\ \times\,8 \\ \hline \end{array} \qquad \begin{array}{r} 6 \\ \times\,8 \\ \hline \end{array} \qquad \begin{array}{r} 4 \\ \times\,8 \\ \hline \end{array} \qquad \begin{array}{r} 8 \\ \times\,8 \\ \hline \end{array}$$

$$\begin{array}{r} 3 \\ \times\,6 \\ \hline \end{array} \qquad \begin{array}{r} 4 \\ \times\,7 \\ \hline \end{array} \qquad \begin{array}{r} 9 \\ \times\,7 \\ \hline \end{array} \qquad \begin{array}{r} 2 \\ \times\,7 \\ \hline \end{array}$$

$$\begin{array}{r} 0 \\ \times\,8 \\ \hline \end{array} \qquad \begin{array}{r} 1 \\ \times\,8 \\ \hline \end{array} \qquad \begin{array}{r} 3 \\ \times\,8 \\ \hline \end{array} \qquad \begin{array}{r} 5 \\ \times\,8 \\ \hline \end{array}$$

Started: _____   Finished: _____   Total Time: _____   Completed: _____   Correct: _____

Name: _____ Date: _____

$$\begin{array}{r} 5 \\ \times\,6 \\ \hline \end{array} \qquad \begin{array}{r} 4 \\ \times\,7 \\ \hline \end{array} \qquad \begin{array}{r} 3 \\ \times\,8 \\ \hline \end{array} \qquad \begin{array}{r} 2 \\ \times\,7 \\ \hline \end{array}$$

$$\begin{array}{r} 2 \\ \times\,8 \\ \hline \end{array} \qquad \begin{array}{r} 3 \\ \times\,6 \\ \hline \end{array} \qquad \begin{array}{r} 8 \\ \times\,7 \\ \hline \end{array} \qquad \begin{array}{r} 5 \\ \times\,8 \\ \hline \end{array}$$

$$\begin{array}{r} 6 \\ \times\,8 \\ \hline \end{array} \qquad \begin{array}{r} 4 \\ \times\,8 \\ \hline \end{array} \qquad \begin{array}{r} 4 \\ \times\,6 \\ \hline \end{array} \qquad \begin{array}{r} 6 \\ \times\,7 \\ \hline \end{array}$$

$$\begin{array}{r} 5 \\ \times\,7 \\ \hline \end{array} \qquad \begin{array}{r} 6 \\ \times\,6 \\ \hline \end{array} \qquad \begin{array}{r} 1 \\ \times\,8 \\ \hline \end{array} \qquad \begin{array}{r} 2 \\ \times\,6 \\ \hline \end{array}$$

$$\begin{array}{r} 8 \\ \times\,6 \\ \hline \end{array} \qquad \begin{array}{r} 3 \\ \times\,7 \\ \hline \end{array} \qquad \begin{array}{r} 7 \\ \times\,7 \\ \hline \end{array} \qquad \begin{array}{r} 7 \\ \times\,8 \\ \hline \end{array}$$

Started: Finished: Total Time: Completed: Correct:

Name: _____   Date: _____

$$\begin{array}{r} 5 \\ \times\,7 \\ \hline \end{array} \qquad \begin{array}{r} 5 \\ \times\,9 \\ \hline \end{array} \qquad \begin{array}{r} 1 \\ \times\,7 \\ \hline \end{array} \qquad \begin{array}{r} 4 \\ \times\,8 \\ \hline \end{array}$$

$$\begin{array}{r} 2 \\ \times\,8 \\ \hline \end{array} \qquad \begin{array}{r} 4 \\ \times\,9 \\ \hline \end{array} \qquad \begin{array}{r} 3 \\ \times\,7 \\ \hline \end{array} \qquad \begin{array}{r} 5 \\ \times\,8 \\ \hline \end{array}$$

$$\begin{array}{r} 9 \\ \times\,7 \\ \hline \end{array} \qquad \begin{array}{r} 6 \\ \times\,9 \\ \hline \end{array} \qquad \begin{array}{r} 7 \\ \times\,7 \\ \hline \end{array} \qquad \begin{array}{r} 9 \\ \times\,8 \\ \hline \end{array}$$

$$\begin{array}{r} 4 \\ \times\,7 \\ \hline \end{array} \qquad \begin{array}{r} 3 \\ \times\,8 \\ \hline \end{array} \qquad \begin{array}{r} 7 \\ \times\,8 \\ \hline \end{array} \qquad \begin{array}{r} 3 \\ \times\,9 \\ \hline \end{array}$$

$$\begin{array}{r} 6 \\ \times\,7 \\ \hline \end{array} \qquad \begin{array}{r} 8 \\ \times\,7 \\ \hline \end{array} \qquad \begin{array}{r} 2 \\ \times\,7 \\ \hline \end{array} \qquad \begin{array}{r} 8 \\ \times\,9 \\ \hline \end{array}$$

Started: Finished: Total Time: Completed: Correct:

Name: _____   Date: _____

3 × 8	2 × 9	4 × 7	8 × 8
5 × 7	9 × 9	6 × 7	7 × 8
9 × 7	6 × 9	7 × 9	4 × 9
8 × 7	5 × 9	7 × 7	1 × 8
2 × 7	5 × 8	6 × 8	4 × 8

Started: _____   Finished: _____   Total Time: _____   Completed: _____   Correct: _____

Name: _____   Date: _____

10 × 6	12 × 2	10 × 7	11 × 5
11 × 6	12 × 3	11 × 7	12 × 8
10 × 1	11 × 9	11 × 3	12 × 9
11 × 2	10 × 9	12 × 4	10 × 3
12 × 6	10 × 8	11 × 4	10 × 5

Started: _____   Finished: _____   Total Time: _____   Completed: _____   Correct: _____

Name: _____   Date: _____

11 × 6	10 × 2	11 ×7	10 × 12
12 × 6	11 × 3	12 × 7	10 × 8
10 × 7	11 × 9	12 × 3	12 × 9
12 × 2	10 × 9	12 × 4	10 × 3
12 × 6	11 × 8	10 × 4	12 × 11

Started: _____ Finished: _____ Total Time: _____ Completed: _____ Correct: _____

Name: _____   Date: _____

12 × 10	12 × 1	11 ×11	12 × 5
10 × 5	11 × 2	12 × 8	11 × 4
10 × 11	11 × 1	10 × 2	11 × 12
10 × 10	12 × 12	12 × 4	11 × 5
11 × 10	10 × 4	12 × 7	11 × 8

Started: _____ Finished: _____ Total Time: _____ Completed: _____ Correct: _____

Name: _____   Date: _____

$$\begin{array}{r} 1 \\ \times\,6 \\ \hline \end{array} \qquad \begin{array}{r} 9 \\ \times\,2 \\ \hline \end{array} \qquad \begin{array}{r} 1 \\ \times\,7 \\ \hline \end{array} \qquad \begin{array}{r} 9 \\ \times\,5 \\ \hline \end{array}$$

$$\begin{array}{r} 5 \\ \times\,6 \\ \hline \end{array} \qquad \begin{array}{r} 5 \\ \times\,3 \\ \hline \end{array} \qquad \begin{array}{r} 8 \\ \times\,7 \\ \hline \end{array} \qquad \begin{array}{r} 4 \\ \times\,8 \\ \hline \end{array}$$

$$\begin{array}{r} 3 \\ \times\,7 \\ \hline \end{array} \qquad \begin{array}{r} 1 \\ \times\,9 \\ \hline \end{array} \qquad \begin{array}{r} 8 \\ \times\,3 \\ \hline \end{array} \qquad \begin{array}{r} 2 \\ \times\,9 \\ \hline \end{array}$$

$$\begin{array}{r} 5 \\ \times\,2 \\ \hline \end{array} \qquad \begin{array}{r} 3 \\ \times\,9 \\ \hline \end{array} \qquad \begin{array}{r} 2 \\ \times\,4 \\ \hline \end{array} \qquad \begin{array}{r} 3 \\ \times\,0 \\ \hline \end{array}$$

$$\begin{array}{r} 2 \\ \times\,6 \\ \hline \end{array} \qquad \begin{array}{r} 9 \\ \times\,8 \\ \hline \end{array} \qquad \begin{array}{r} 8 \\ \times\,4 \\ \hline \end{array} \qquad \begin{array}{r} 5 \\ \times\,9 \\ \hline \end{array}$$

Started: Finished: Total Time: Completed: Correct:

Name: _____ Date: _____

$$8 \times 3 \qquad 2 \times 9 \qquad 4 \times 7 \qquad 8 \times 8$$

$$7 \times 5 \qquad 9 \times 9 \qquad 6 \times 7 \qquad 7 \times 8$$

$$9 \times 7 \qquad 6 \times 9 \qquad 7 \times 9 \qquad 9 \times 4$$

$$8 \times 7 \qquad 9 \times 5 \qquad 7 \times 7 \qquad 1 \times 8$$

$$8 \times 2 \qquad 8 \times 5 \qquad 6 \times 8 \qquad 3 \times 9$$

Started: Finished: Total Time: Completed: Correct: _____

Name: _____   Date: _____

$$\begin{array}{r} 7 \\ \times\,2 \\ \hline \end{array} \qquad \begin{array}{r} 8 \\ \times\,1 \\ \hline \end{array} \qquad \begin{array}{r} 6 \\ \times\,3 \\ \hline \end{array} \qquad \begin{array}{r} 8 \\ \times\,8 \\ \hline \end{array}$$

$$\begin{array}{r} 6 \\ \times\,4 \\ \hline \end{array} \qquad \begin{array}{r} 9 \\ \times\,9 \\ \hline \end{array} \qquad \begin{array}{r} 6 \\ \times\,5 \\ \hline \end{array} \qquad \begin{array}{r} 2 \\ \times\,6 \\ \hline \end{array}$$

$$\begin{array}{r} 7 \\ \times\,5 \\ \hline \end{array} \qquad \begin{array}{r} 7 \\ \times\,4 \\ \hline \end{array} \qquad \begin{array}{r} 9 \\ \times\,5 \\ \hline \end{array} \qquad \begin{array}{r} 8 \\ \times\,3 \\ \hline \end{array}$$

$$\begin{array}{r} 4 \\ \times\,5 \\ \hline \end{array} \qquad \begin{array}{r} 2 \\ \times\,4 \\ \hline \end{array} \qquad \begin{array}{r} 7 \\ \times\,3 \\ \hline \end{array} \qquad \begin{array}{r} 9 \\ \times\,2 \\ \hline \end{array}$$

$$\begin{array}{r} 8 \\ \times\,7 \\ \hline \end{array} \qquad \begin{array}{r} 9 \\ \times\,4 \\ \hline \end{array} \qquad \begin{array}{r} 8 \\ \times\,6 \\ \hline \end{array} \qquad \begin{array}{r} 9 \\ \times\,6 \\ \hline \end{array}$$

Started: _____   Finished: _____   Total Time: _____   Completed: _____   Correct: _____

Name: _____   Date: _____

$$\begin{array}{r} 3 \\ \times\,8 \\ \hline \end{array} \qquad \begin{array}{r} 2 \\ \times\,9 \\ \hline \end{array} \qquad \begin{array}{r} 4 \\ \times\,2 \\ \hline \end{array} \qquad \begin{array}{r} 8 \\ \times\,5 \\ \hline \end{array}$$

$$\begin{array}{r} 5 \\ \times\,7 \\ \hline \end{array} \qquad \begin{array}{r} 9 \\ \times\,8 \\ \hline \end{array} \qquad \begin{array}{r} 6 \\ \times\,7 \\ \hline \end{array} \qquad \begin{array}{r} 7 \\ \times\,3 \\ \hline \end{array}$$

$$\begin{array}{r} 9 \\ \times\,3 \\ \hline \end{array} \qquad \begin{array}{r} 6 \\ \times\,5 \\ \hline \end{array} \qquad \begin{array}{r} 7 \\ \times\,9 \\ \hline \end{array} \qquad \begin{array}{r} 4 \\ \times\,9 \\ \hline \end{array}$$

$$\begin{array}{r} 8 \\ \times\,7 \\ \hline \end{array} \qquad \begin{array}{r} 5 \\ \times\,9 \\ \hline \end{array} \qquad \begin{array}{r} 6 \\ \times\,6 \\ \hline \end{array} \qquad \begin{array}{r} 1 \\ \times\,8 \\ \hline \end{array}$$

$$\begin{array}{r} 8 \\ \times\,4 \\ \hline \end{array} \qquad \begin{array}{r} 4 \\ \times\,3 \\ \hline \end{array} \qquad \begin{array}{r} 4 \\ \times\,7 \\ \hline \end{array} \qquad \begin{array}{r} 7 \\ \times\,8 \\ \hline \end{array}$$

Started: Finished: Total Time: Completed: Correct:

Name: _____   Date: _____

$$\begin{array}{r} 8 \\ \times 3 \\ \hline \end{array} \qquad \begin{array}{r} 7 \\ \times 6 \\ \hline \end{array} \qquad \begin{array}{r} 3 \\ \times 8 \\ \hline \end{array} \qquad \begin{array}{r} 9 \\ \times 3 \\ \hline \end{array} \qquad \begin{array}{r} 9 \\ \times 5 \\ \hline \end{array}$$

$$\begin{array}{r} 5 \\ \times 5 \\ \hline \end{array} \qquad \begin{array}{r} 5 \\ \times 8 \\ \hline \end{array} \qquad \begin{array}{r} 8 \\ \times 6 \\ \hline \end{array} \qquad \begin{array}{r} 7 \\ \times 9 \\ \hline \end{array} \qquad \begin{array}{r} 6 \\ \times 7 \\ \hline \end{array}$$

$$\begin{array}{r} 8 \\ \times 2 \\ \hline \end{array} \qquad \begin{array}{r} 4 \\ \times 7 \\ \hline \end{array} \qquad \begin{array}{r} 5 \\ \times 3 \\ \hline \end{array} \qquad \begin{array}{r} 3 \\ \times 1 \\ \hline \end{array} \qquad \begin{array}{r} 7 \\ \times 8 \\ \hline \end{array}$$

$$\begin{array}{r} 5 \\ \times 6 \\ \hline \end{array} \qquad \begin{array}{r} 3 \\ \times 5 \\ \hline \end{array} \qquad \begin{array}{r} 7 \\ \times 7 \\ \hline \end{array} \qquad \begin{array}{r} 9 \\ \times 4 \\ \hline \end{array} \qquad \begin{array}{r} 6 \\ \times 3 \\ \hline \end{array}$$

$$\begin{array}{r} 5 \\ \times 4 \\ \hline \end{array} \qquad \begin{array}{r} 7 \\ \times 4 \\ \hline \end{array} \qquad \begin{array}{r} 9 \\ \times 0 \\ \hline \end{array} \qquad \begin{array}{r} 6 \\ \times 8 \\ \hline \end{array} \qquad \begin{array}{r} 8 \\ \times 9 \\ \hline \end{array}$$

$$\begin{array}{r} 2 \\ \times 6 \\ \hline \end{array} \qquad \begin{array}{r} 4 \\ \times 2 \\ \hline \end{array} \qquad \begin{array}{r} 9 \\ \times 7 \\ \hline \end{array} \qquad \begin{array}{r} 9 \\ \times 9 \\ \hline \end{array} \qquad \begin{array}{r} 6 \\ \times 5 \\ \hline \end{array}$$

Started: Finished: Total Time: Completed: Correct:

Name: _____   Date: _____

1 ×1	9 ×2	4 ×3	3 ×4	5 ×5
6 ×6	5 ×7	8 ×8	9 ×9	7 ×2
2 ×3	4 ×4	6 ×5	3 ×6	7 ×7
5 ×8	5 ×9	8 ×1	4 ×2	7 ×3
8 ×4	7 ×5	2 ×6	3 ×7	8 ×0
8 ×9	1 ×4	8 ×5	4 ×6	9 ×7

Started: _____   Finished: _____   Total Time: _____   Completed: _____   Correct: _____

Name: _____   Date: _____

2 × 8	5 × 6	4 × 8	4 × 0	5 × 4
7 × 6	6 × 8	6 × 2	8 × 9	7 × 4
6 × 7	4 × 3	7 × 5	4 × 7	7 × 8
6 × 6	1 × 7	9 × 8	6 × 9	8 × 6
6 × 3	8 × 3	6 × 1	3 × 8	7 × 9
8 × 2	3 × 9	9 × 7	6 × 4	3 × 2

Started: _____ Finished: _____ Total Time: _____ Completed: _____ Correct: _____

Name: _____   Date: _____

5 × 1	4 × 5	9 × 3	9 × 8	8 × 4
2 × 6	1 × 8	8 × 6	5 × 8	7 × 7
5 × 7	5 × 2	3 × 5	4 × 1	9 × 6
5 × 6	2 × 7	8 × 9	4 × 9	5 × 3
6 × 0	9 × 1	3 × 3	5 × 9	3 × 7
2 × 2	3 × 9	2 × 5	6 × 4	8 × 5

Started: Finished: Total Time: Completed: Correct:

Name: _____   Date: _____

7 ×6	2 ×7	4 ×4	5 ×5	3 ×8
5 ×8	1 ×5	9 ×7	4 ×9	3 ×3
5 ×6	6 ×8	5 ×3	8 ×9	6 ×7
8 ×6	8 ×8	7 ×5	2 ×2	3 ×9
7 ×3	5 ×7	1 ×6	6 ×9	4 ×0
3 ×7	6 ×6	5 ×2	3 ×5	7 ×4

Started: _____   Finished: _____   Total Time: _____   Completed: _____   Correct: _____

Name: _____   Date: _____

2 ×6	4 ×7	4 ×8	2 ×9	6 ×2
6 ×3	6 ×7	8 ×6	9 ×1	5 ×6
2 ×3	3 ×4	6 ×5	3 ×6	7 ×7
5 ×8	4 ×5	8 ×4	5 ×9	3 ×3
6 ×4	8 ×5	2 ×0	3 ×7	8 ×0
3 ×9	1 ×4	3 ×5	4 ×6	5 ×7
6 ×1	4 ×2	4 ×3	2 ×4	2 ×5
7 ×8	7 ×9	3 ×1	9 ×9	8 ×2

Started: _____ Finished: _____ Total Time: _____ Completed: _____ Correct: _____

Name: _____   Date: _____

3 × 6	5 × 7	6 × 8	3 × 9	7 × 2
6 × 4	4 × 8	8 × 7	9 × 2	2 × 7
3 × 3	4 × 4	5 × 5	6 × 6	7 × 7
3 × 8	7 × 5	8 × 4	5 × 9	3 × 5
7 × 4	4 × 2	4 × 3	2 × 4	2 × 5
8 × 8	7 × 9	3 × 1	9 × 9	8 × 6
6 × 2	8 × 5	2 × 6	3 × 7	8 × 0
6 × 9	5 × 0	4 × 5	4 × 6	4 × 7

Started: _____   Finished: _____   Total Time: _____   Completed: _____   Correct: _____

Name: _____   Date: _____

7 × 6	7 × 8	3 × 8	9 × 9	8 × 2
5 × 3	4 × 7	9 × 6	9 × 1	5 × 6
2 × 3	3 × 4	4 × 5	3 × 6	9 × 7
2 × 8	6 × 5	8 × 4	4 × 9	7 × 3
5 × 4	9 × 5	6 × 6	3 × 7	8 × 0
3 × 9	1 × 4	8 × 5	4 × 6	0 × 7
5 × 8	5 × 9	6 × 1	2 × 9	5 × 2
3 × 3	3 × 2	9 × 8	9 × 4	8 × 1

Started: _____   Finished: _____   Total Time: _____   Completed: _____   Correct: _____

Name: _____   Date: _____

5 × 4	4 × 8	4 × 7	2 × 2	2 × 7
3 × 8	7 × 5	8 × 4	5 × 9	3 × 5
3 × 6	7 × 3	2 × 8	7 × 9	7 × 2
6 × 3	5 × 2	8 × 8	3 × 4	5 × 1
3 × 3	4 × 4	5 × 5	6 × 6	7 × 7
7 × 4	4 × 2	4 × 3	2 × 4	2 × 5
6 × 2	6 × 5	2 × 6	4 × 5	3 × 0
5 × 8	5 × 6	6 × 4	9 × 4	8 × 2

Started: _____ Finished: _____ Total Time: _____ Completed: _____ Correct: _____

Name: _____   Date: _____

6 × 3	5 × 4	9 × 5	4 × 6	6 × 7
7 × 0	3 × 2	6 × 4	5 × 6	7 × 8
9 × 3	8 × 4	2 × 5	8 × 6	8 × 7
6 × 9	5 × 0	6 × 5	3 × 4	4 × 7
8 × 0	5 × 2	9 × 4	8 × 2	2 × 8
3 × 3	7 × 4	5 × 5	2 × 6	3 × 7
9 × 9	6 × 1	7 × 5	6 × 6	5 × 7
6 × 2	4 × 4	8 × 5	3 × 6	7 × 7

Started: _____   Finished: _____   Total Time: _____   Completed: _____   Correct: _____

Name: _____   Date: _____

$$\begin{array}{r} 5 \\ \times\, 3 \\ \hline \end{array} \qquad \begin{array}{r} 8 \\ \times\, 4 \\ \hline \end{array} \qquad \begin{array}{r} 3 \\ \times\, 5 \\ \hline \end{array} \qquad \begin{array}{r} 7 \\ \times\, 6 \\ \hline \end{array} \qquad \begin{array}{r} 8 \\ \times\, 3 \\ \hline \end{array}$$

$$\begin{array}{r} 2 \\ \times\, 6 \\ \hline \end{array} \qquad \begin{array}{r} 4 \\ \times\, 7 \\ \hline \end{array} \qquad \begin{array}{r} 4 \\ \times\, 8 \\ \hline \end{array} \qquad \begin{array}{r} 2 \\ \times\, 9 \\ \hline \end{array} \qquad \begin{array}{r} 6 \\ \times\, 2 \\ \hline \end{array}$$

$$\begin{array}{r} 5 \\ \times\, 6 \\ \hline \end{array} \qquad \begin{array}{r} 6 \\ \times\, 3 \\ \hline \end{array} \qquad \begin{array}{r} 8 \\ \times\, 7 \\ \hline \end{array} \qquad \begin{array}{r} 8 \\ \times\, 6 \\ \hline \end{array} \qquad \begin{array}{r} 9 \\ \times\, 1 \\ \hline \end{array}$$

$$\begin{array}{r} 7 \\ \times\, 3 \\ \hline \end{array} \qquad \begin{array}{r} 2 \\ \times\, 4 \\ \hline \end{array} \qquad \begin{array}{r} 6 \\ \times\, 5 \\ \hline \end{array} \qquad \begin{array}{r} 6 \\ \times\, 6 \\ \hline \end{array} \qquad \begin{array}{r} 3 \\ \times\, 7 \\ \hline \end{array}$$

$$\begin{array}{r} 5 \\ \times\, 8 \\ \hline \end{array} \qquad \begin{array}{r} 4 \\ \times\, 5 \\ \hline \end{array} \qquad \begin{array}{r} 3 \\ \times\, 4 \\ \hline \end{array} \qquad \begin{array}{r} 5 \\ \times\, 9 \\ \hline \end{array} \qquad \begin{array}{r} 3 \\ \times\, 3 \\ \hline \end{array}$$

$$\begin{array}{r} 6 \\ \times\, 4 \\ \hline \end{array} \qquad \begin{array}{r} 8 \\ \times\, 5 \\ \hline \end{array} \qquad \begin{array}{r} 4 \\ \times\, 6 \\ \hline \end{array} \qquad \begin{array}{r} 7 \\ \times\, 7 \\ \hline \end{array} \qquad \begin{array}{r} 6 \\ \times\, 0 \\ \hline \end{array}$$

$$\begin{array}{r} 9 \\ \times\, 5 \\ \hline \end{array} \qquad \begin{array}{r} 4 \\ \times\, 0 \\ \hline \end{array} \qquad \begin{array}{r} 7 \\ \times\, 5 \\ \hline \end{array} \qquad \begin{array}{r} 3 \\ \times\, 6 \\ \hline \end{array} \qquad \begin{array}{r} 5 \\ \times\, 7 \\ \hline \end{array}$$

$$\begin{array}{r} 4 \\ \times\, 9 \\ \hline \end{array} \qquad \begin{array}{r} 9 \\ \times\, 2 \\ \hline \end{array} \qquad \begin{array}{r} 4 \\ \times\, 3 \\ \hline \end{array} \qquad \begin{array}{r} 2 \\ \times\, 5 \\ \hline \end{array} \qquad \begin{array}{r} 4 \\ \times\, 4 \\ \hline \end{array}$$

$$\begin{array}{r} 7 \\ \times\, 8 \\ \hline \end{array} \qquad \begin{array}{r} 7 \\ \times\, 9 \\ \hline \end{array} \qquad \begin{array}{r} 3 \\ \times\, 1 \\ \hline \end{array} \qquad \begin{array}{r} 9 \\ \times\, 9 \\ \hline \end{array} \qquad \begin{array}{r} 8 \\ \times\, 2 \\ \hline \end{array}$$

$$\begin{array}{r} 9 \\ \times\, 3 \\ \hline \end{array} \qquad \begin{array}{r} 6 \\ \times\, 7 \\ \hline \end{array} \qquad \begin{array}{r} 8 \\ \times\, 8 \\ \hline \end{array} \qquad \begin{array}{r} 7 \\ \times\, 1 \\ \hline \end{array} \qquad \begin{array}{r} 3 \\ \times\, 8 \\ \hline \end{array}$$

Started: _____   Finished: _____   Total Time: _____   Completed: _____   Correct: _____

Name: _____   Date: _____

8 × 3	5 × 4	8 × 5	3 × 6	7 × 3
8 × 6	2 × 7	4 × 8	3 × 9	2 × 2
9 × 6	2 × 3	9 × 7	5 × 6	8 × 0
9 × 3	7 × 4	5 × 5	6 × 6	6 × 7
3 × 8	3 × 5	4 × 4	6 × 9	5 × 3
9 × 4	6 × 5	6 × 4	4 × 7	4 × 0
6 × 8	9 × 1	4 × 5	7 × 6	3 × 7
5 × 9	4 × 2	4 × 3	2 × 8	2 × 4
5 × 8	7 × 9	6 × 1	9 × 9	9 × 2
8 × 8	7 × 2	2 × 6	0 × 1	8 × 9

Started: Finished: Total Time: Completed: Correct:

Name: _____   Date: _____

$$\begin{array}{r} 5 \\ \times 2 \\ \hline \end{array} \qquad \begin{array}{r} 4 \\ \times 8 \\ \hline \end{array} \qquad \begin{array}{r} 3 \\ \times 5 \\ \hline \end{array} \qquad \begin{array}{r} 5 \\ \times 4 \\ \hline \end{array} \qquad \begin{array}{r} 3 \\ \times 9 \\ \hline \end{array}$$

$$\begin{array}{r} 5 \\ \times 3 \\ \hline \end{array} \qquad \begin{array}{r} 8 \\ \times 4 \\ \hline \end{array} \qquad \begin{array}{r} 6 \\ \times 5 \\ \hline \end{array} \qquad \begin{array}{r} 7 \\ \times 6 \\ \hline \end{array} \qquad \begin{array}{r} 8 \\ \times 3 \\ \hline \end{array}$$

$$\begin{array}{r} 2 \\ \times 3 \\ \hline \end{array} \qquad \begin{array}{r} 4 \\ \times 6 \\ \hline \end{array} \qquad \begin{array}{r} 4 \\ \times 7 \\ \hline \end{array} \qquad \begin{array}{r} 2 \\ \times 8 \\ \hline \end{array} \qquad \begin{array}{r} 6 \\ \times 9 \\ \hline \end{array}$$

$$\begin{array}{r} 5 \\ \times 6 \\ \hline \end{array} \qquad \begin{array}{r} 6 \\ \times 3 \\ \hline \end{array} \qquad \begin{array}{r} 8 \\ \times 7 \\ \hline \end{array} \qquad \begin{array}{r} 8 \\ \times 6 \\ \hline \end{array} \qquad \begin{array}{r} 9 \\ \times 1 \\ \hline \end{array}$$

$$\begin{array}{r} 5 \\ \times 7 \\ \hline \end{array} \qquad \begin{array}{r} 6 \\ \times 8 \\ \hline \end{array} \qquad \begin{array}{r} 3 \\ \times 3 \\ \hline \end{array} \qquad \begin{array}{r} 4 \\ \times 4 \\ \hline \end{array} \qquad \begin{array}{r} 4 \\ \times 9 \\ \hline \end{array}$$

$$\begin{array}{r} 6 \\ \times 4 \\ \hline \end{array} \qquad \begin{array}{r} 8 \\ \times 5 \\ \hline \end{array} \qquad \begin{array}{r} 3 \\ \times 6 \\ \hline \end{array} \qquad \begin{array}{r} 7 \\ \times 7 \\ \hline \end{array} \qquad \begin{array}{r} 6 \\ \times 0 \\ \hline \end{array}$$

$$\begin{array}{r} 9 \\ \times 3 \\ \hline \end{array} \qquad \begin{array}{r} 4 \\ \times 5 \\ \hline \end{array} \qquad \begin{array}{r} 7 \\ \times 0 \\ \hline \end{array} \qquad \begin{array}{r} 7 \\ \times 5 \\ \hline \end{array} \qquad \begin{array}{r} 6 \\ \times 6 \\ \hline \end{array}$$

$$\begin{array}{r} 7 \\ \times 3 \\ \hline \end{array} \qquad \begin{array}{r} 3 \\ \times 2 \\ \hline \end{array} \qquad \begin{array}{r} 7 \\ \times 4 \\ \hline \end{array} \qquad \begin{array}{r} 5 \\ \times 5 \\ \hline \end{array} \qquad \begin{array}{r} 3 \\ \times 7 \\ \hline \end{array}$$

$$\begin{array}{r} 5 \\ \times 9 \\ \hline \end{array} \qquad \begin{array}{r} 9 \\ \times 2 \\ \hline \end{array} \qquad \begin{array}{r} 4 \\ \times 3 \\ \hline \end{array} \qquad \begin{array}{r} 2 \\ \times 5 \\ \hline \end{array} \qquad \begin{array}{r} 3 \\ \times 4 \\ \hline \end{array}$$

$$\begin{array}{r} 1 \\ \times 3 \\ \hline \end{array} \qquad \begin{array}{r} 6 \\ \times 7 \\ \hline \end{array} \qquad \begin{array}{r} 8 \\ \times 8 \\ \hline \end{array} \qquad \begin{array}{r} 9 \\ \times 9 \\ \hline \end{array} \qquad \begin{array}{r} 2 \\ \times 9 \\ \hline \end{array}$$

Started: _____ Finished: _____ Total Time: _____ Completed: _____ Correct: _____

Name: _____ Date: _____

2 ×3	6 ×4	5 ×5	8 ×6	3 ×3
8 ×1	9 ×7	2 ×4	9 ×9	6 ×2
5 ×6	6 ×3	8 ×7	9 ×6	9 ×1
7 ×3	4 ×4	6 ×5	6 ×6	2 ×7
5 ×8	4 ×5	3 ×4	5 ×9	8 ×3
7 ×4	8 ×5	2 ×6	7 ×7	0 ×4
9 ×5	4 ×1	7 ×5	0 ×6	5 ×7
4 ×9	7 ×2	4 ×2	2 ×5	9 ×4
9 ×8	7 ×9	3 ×1	2 ×9	8 ×2
9 ×3	6 ×7	8 ×8	7 ×0	4 ×8

Started: _____ Finished: _____ Total Time: _____ Completed: _____ Correct: _____

Name: _____ Date: _____

5 ×8	8 ×9	3 ×0	7 ×9	8 ×2
3 ×6	4 ×7	8 ×8	6 ×9	7 ×2
8 ×3	5 ×4	6 ×5	9 ×6	7 ×7
5 ×2	4 ×5	8 ×4	5 ×9	3 ×3
6 ×4	8 ×5	2 ×6	3 ×7	8 ×0
5 ×3	1 ×4	7 ×5	4 ×6	7 ×3
6 ×1	4 ×2	4 ×3	2 ×4	5 ×5
4 ×9	7 ×4	3 ×5	7 ×6	8 ×7
6 ×3	5 ×7	8 ×6	6 ×7	5 ×6
9 ×3	3 ×8	6 ×6	9 ×1	2 ×9

Started: _____ Finished: _____ Total Time: _____ Completed: _____ Correct: _____

Name: _____   Date: _____

9 × 3	2 × 8	6 × 6	8 × 1	3 × 9
3 × 6	4 × 7	8 × 3	6 × 9	6 × 2
9 × 2	2 × 5	4 × 4	8 × 0	3 × 2
4 × 8	7 × 9	5 × 1	9 × 9	2 × 2
6 × 8	7 × 3	2 × 7	4 × 1	4 × 9
5 × 6	8 × 2	4 × 3	5 × 5	3 × 4
4 × 6	7 × 4	3 × 5	7 × 6	8 × 7
9 × 6	8 × 5	9 × 4	2 × 3	5 × 2
6 × 3	8 × 4	6 × 5	8 × 6	7 × 7
5 × 7	8 × 8	6 × 4	5 × 9	3 × 3

Started: _____   Finished: _____   Total Time: _____   Completed: _____   Correct: _____

Name: _____   Date: _____

$5 \div 1 =$ $10 \div 2 =$

$9 \div 3 =$ $16 \div 4 =$

$5 \div 5 =$ $12 \div 3 =$

$8 \div 2 =$ $15 \div 3 =$

$6 \div 1 =$ $2 \div 2 =$

$20 \div 5 =$ $3 \div 1 =$

$14 \div 2 =$ $25 \div 5 =$

$35 \div 5 =$ $8 \div 4 =$

$4 \div 1 =$ $20 \div 2 =$

$45 \div 5 =$ $16 \div 2 =$

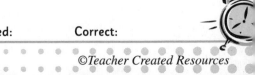

Started: Finished: Total Time: Completed: Correct:

Name: _____   Date: _____

$4\overline{)32}$ $2\overline{)16}$ $2\overline{)6}$ $1\overline{)7}$

$5\overline{)15}$ $2\overline{)10}$ $5\overline{)25}$ $2\overline{)18}$

$5\overline{)5}$ $5\overline{)10}$ $4\overline{)8}$ $4\overline{)4}$

$3\overline{)12}$ $5\overline{)35}$ $1\overline{)9}$ $5\overline{)45}$

$1\overline{)4}$ $2\overline{)8}$ $4\overline{)40}$ $3\overline{)21}$

Started: Finished: Total Time: Completed: Correct:

Name: _____   Date: _____

$8 \div 2 =$ $18 \div 3 =$

$10 \div 2 =$ $30 \div 5 =$

$9 \div 1 =$ $20 \div 2 =$

$4 \div 2 =$ $5 \div 1 =$

$10 \div 5 =$ $8 \div 4 =$

$21 \div 3 =$ $9 \div 3 =$

$16 \div 2 =$ $6 \div 3 =$

$20 \div 4 =$ $15 \div 5 =$

$12 \div 4 =$ $12 \div 2 =$

$16 \div 4 =$ $3 \div 3 =$

Started: Finished: Total Time: Completed: Correct:

Name: _____   Date: _____

$3\overline{)9}$ $5\overline{)40}$ $1\overline{)7}$ $5\overline{)25}$

$2\overline{)10}$ $5\overline{)30}$ $2\overline{)12}$ $4\overline{)12}$

$3\overline{)24}$ $1\overline{)6}$ $2\overline{)16}$ $5\overline{)20}$

$2\overline{)8}$ $5\overline{)35}$ $4\overline{)16}$ $4\overline{)32}$

$3\overline{)15}$ $3\overline{)12}$ $4\overline{)20}$ $1\overline{)3}$

Started: Finished: Total Time: Completed: Correct:

Name: _____   Date: _____

$6 \div 3 =$ $28 \div 4 =$ $8 \div 2 =$

$3 \div 1 =$ $40 \div 5 =$ $4 \div 4 =$

$9 \div 3 =$ $18 \div 2 =$ $8 \div 4 =$

$10 \div 5 =$ $12 \div 4 =$ $12 \div 3 =$

$7 \div 1 =$ $12 \div 2 =$ $20 \div 5 =$

$15 \div 3 =$ $36 \div 4 =$ $21 \div 3 =$

$15 \div 5 =$ $16 \div 2 =$ $14 \div 2 =$

$16 \div 4 =$ $25 \div 5 =$ $2 \div 2 =$

$24 \div 3 =$ $5 \div 1 =$ $10 \div 2 =$

$18 \div 3 =$ $20 \div 4 =$ $4 \div 1 =$

Started: _____   Finished: _____   Total Time: _____   Completed: _____   Correct: _____

Name: _____   Date: _____

$3\overline{)6}$ $2\overline{)12}$ $5\overline{)20}$ $1\overline{)3}$ $4\overline{)8}$

$4\overline{)32}$ $3\overline{)27}$ $5\overline{)15}$ $2\overline{)10}$ $1\overline{)8}$

$2\overline{)16}$ $3\overline{)18}$ $4\overline{)24}$ $5\overline{)5}$ $3\overline{)12}$

$2\overline{)14}$ $5\overline{)30}$ $3\overline{)15}$ $1\overline{)7}$ $5\overline{)35}$

$2\overline{)8}$ $4\overline{)36}$ $5\overline{)10}$ $3\overline{)9}$ $1\overline{)1}$

$5\overline{)25}$ $3\overline{)24}$ $1\overline{)9}$ $2\overline{)18}$ $2\overline{)6}$

Started: _____   Finished: _____   Total Time: _____   Completed: _____   Correct: _____

Name: _____ Date: _____

$$5 \div 5 =$$ $$6 \div 1 =$$ $$12 \div 3 =$$

$$8 \div 4 =$$ $$8 \div 2 =$$ $$4 \div 4 =$$

$$6 \div 2 =$$ $$4 \div 1 =$$ $$25 \div 5 =$$

$$15 \div 5 =$$ $$3 \div 3 =$$ $$18 \div 3 =$$

$$40 \div 5 =$$ $$2 \div 1 =$$ $$28 \div 4 =$$

$$2 \div 2 =$$ $$24 \div 4 =$$ $$16 \div 4 =$$

$$15 \div 3 =$$ $$6 \div 3 =$$ $$1 \div 1 =$$

$$30 \div 5 =$$ $$32 \div 4 =$$ $$21 \div 3 =$$

$$20 \div 5 =$$ $$16 \div 2 =$$ $$20 \div 4 =$$

$$10 \div 5 =$$ $$9 \div 3 =$$ $$35 \div 5 =$$

Started: Finished: Total Time: Completed: Correct:

Name: _____   Date: _____

$5 \overline{)5}$ $4 \overline{)20}$ $3 \overline{)3}$ $2 \overline{)16}$ $1 \overline{)9}$

$4 \overline{)12}$ $2 \overline{)12}$ $3 \overline{)9}$ $5 \overline{)35}$ $3 \overline{)12}$

$5 \overline{)20}$ $3 \overline{)15}$ $2 \overline{)4}$ $4 \overline{)36}$ $3 \overline{)21}$

$2 \overline{)8}$ $3 \overline{)18}$ $5 \overline{)15}$ $2 \overline{)18}$ $4 \overline{)16}$

$1 \overline{)4}$ $3 \overline{)27}$ $5 \overline{)10}$ $2 \overline{)10}$ $4 \overline{)8}$

$5 \overline{)25}$ $4 \overline{)24}$ $3 \overline{)24}$ $4 \overline{)28}$ $1 \overline{)6}$

Started: _____ Finished: _____ Total Time: _____ Completed: _____ Correct: _____

Name: _____   Date: _____

$18 \div 6 =$

$0 \div 8 =$

$24 \div 8 =$

$27 \div 9 =$

$48 \div 6 =$

$32 \div 8 =$

$36 \div 9 =$

$30 \div 6 =$

$16 \div 8 =$

$54 \div 9 =$

$56 \div 7 =$

$18 \div 9 =$

$35 \div 7 =$

$24 \div 6 =$

$0 \div 7 =$

$9 \div 9 =$

$72 \div 8 =$

$49 \div 7 =$

$7 \div 7 =$

$12 \div 6 =$

Started: _____   Finished: _____   Total Time: _____   Completed: _____   Correct: _____

Name: _____   Date: _____

$6\overline{)12}$ $8\overline{)8}$ $7\overline{)49}$ $6\overline{)6}$

$9\overline{)45}$ $6\overline{)48}$ $7\overline{)21}$ $8\overline{)40}$

$8\overline{)24}$ $7\overline{)14}$ $6\overline{)36}$ $9\overline{)0}$

$9\overline{)27}$ $8\overline{)48}$ $9\overline{)81}$ $6\overline{)42}$

$6\overline{)18}$ $7\overline{)7}$ $6\overline{)24}$ $7\overline{)28}$

Started: _____   Finished: _____   Total Time: _____   Completed: _____   Correct: _____

Name: _____   Date: _____

$40 \div 8 =$ $42 \div 7 =$

$64 \div 8 =$ $18 \div 9 =$

$63 \div 7 =$ $54 \div 6 =$

$16 \div 8 =$ $9 \div 9 =$

$35 \div 7 =$ $54 \div 9 =$

$48 \div 6 =$ $56 \div 8 =$

$24 \div 6 =$ $28 \div 7 =$

$72 \div 8 =$ $27 \div 9 =$

$30 \div 6 =$ $72 \div 9 =$

$32 \div 8 =$ $49 \div 7 =$

Started: _____   Finished: _____   Total Time: _____   Completed: _____   Correct: _____

Name: _____ Date: _____

$6\overline{)42}$ $7\overline{)21}$ $8\overline{)72}$ $9\overline{)27}$

$7\overline{)28}$ $9\overline{)18}$ $6\overline{)36}$ $8\overline{)8}$

$8\overline{)32}$ $6\overline{)54}$ $7\overline{)0}$ $9\overline{)36}$

$9\overline{)72}$ $8\overline{)24}$ $6\overline{)6}$ $7\overline{)63}$

$6\overline{)48}$ $7\overline{)14}$ $8\overline{)16}$ $9\overline{)54}$

Started: Finished: Total Time: Completed: Correct:

Name: _____   Date: _____

$18 \div 9 =$ $36 \div 9 =$ $32 \div 8 =$

$48 \div 8 =$ $36 \div 6 =$ $63 \div 7 =$

$64 \div 8 =$ $12 \div 6 =$ $16 \div 8 =$

$63 \div 9 =$ $24 \div 8 =$ $45 \div 9 =$

$28 \div 7 =$ $54 \div 9 =$ $24 \div 6 =$

$14 \div 7 =$ $54 \div 6 =$ $49 \div 7 =$

$9 \div 9 =$ $56 \div 7 =$ $18 \div 6 =$

$21 \div 7 =$ $56 \div 8 =$ $42 \div 6 =$

$81 \div 9 =$ $27 \div 9 =$ $40 \div 8 =$

$6 \div 6 =$ $35 \div 7 =$ $48 \div 6 =$

Started: Finished: Total Time: Completed: Correct:

Name: _____   Date: _____

$6\overline{)30}$ $7\overline{)35}$ $9\overline{)63}$ $6\overline{)48}$ $8\overline{)40}$

$7\overline{)56}$ $6\overline{)36}$ $8\overline{)48}$ $8\overline{)64}$ $9\overline{)9}$

$6\overline{)42}$ $7\overline{)21}$ $7\overline{)28}$ $8\overline{)72}$ $9\overline{)27}$

$8\overline{)32}$ $9\overline{)72}$ $6\overline{)54}$ $7\overline{)49}$ $9\overline{)36}$

$9\overline{)54}$ $8\overline{)24}$ $6\overline{)18}$ $6\overline{)6}$ $7\overline{)63}$

$6\overline{)12}$ $9\overline{)18}$ $7\overline{)14}$ $8\overline{)16}$ $9\overline{)45}$

Started: _____   Finished: _____   Total Time: _____   Completed: _____   Correct: _____

Name: _____   Date: _____

$18 \div 6 =$ $7 \div 7 =$ $24 \div 8 =$

$42 \div 7 =$ $18 \div 9 =$ $8 \div 8 =$

$40 \div 8 =$ $21 \div 7 =$ $24 \div 6 =$

$35 \div 7 =$ $48 \div 6 =$ $63 \div 7 =$

$54 \div 6 =$ $72 \div 8 =$ $54 \div 9 =$

$28 \div 7 =$ $32 \div 8 =$ $36 \div 9 =$

$56 \div 8 =$ $36 \div 6 =$ $64 \div 8 =$

$45 \div 9 =$ $63 \div 9 =$ $48 \div 8 =$

$49 \div 7 =$ $27 \div 9 =$ $14 \div 7 =$

$16 \div 8 =$ $72 \div 9 =$ $30 \div 6 =$

Started: _____   Finished: _____   Total Time: _____   Completed: _____   Correct: _____

Name: _____   Date: _____

$8 \overline{)16}$ $6 \overline{)6}$ $7 \overline{)21}$ $9 \overline{)81}$ $8 \overline{)56}$

$9 \overline{)9}$ $8 \overline{)72}$ $7 \overline{)7}$ $6 \overline{)18}$ $9 \overline{)54}$

$6 \overline{)12}$ $7 \overline{)49}$ $9 \overline{)45}$ $8 \overline{)8}$ $6 \overline{)30}$

$9 \overline{)27}$ $8 \overline{)24}$ $7 \overline{)63}$ $6 \overline{)42}$ $9 \overline{)27}$

$7 \overline{)14}$ $6 \overline{)54}$ $9 \overline{)36}$ $7 \overline{)35}$ $6 \overline{)48}$

$6 \overline{)24}$ $8 \overline{)40}$ $7 \overline{)56}$ $8 \overline{)64}$ $9 \overline{)18}$

Started: _____ Finished: _____ Total Time: _____ Completed: _____ Correct: _____

Name: _____   Date: _____

$36 \div 9 =$ $16 \div 4 =$

$12 \div 2 =$ $30 \div 5 =$

$54 \div 9 =$ $8 \div 1 =$

$28 \div 7 =$ $24 \div 8 =$

$16 \div 8 =$ $45 \div 5 =$

$30 \div 6 =$ $49 \div 7 =$

$24 \div 3 =$ $18 \div 2 =$

$63 \div 7 =$ $32 \div 4 =$

$24 \div 4 =$ $27 \div 3 =$

$54 \div 6 =$ $40 \div 5 =$

Started: Finished: Total Time: Completed: Correct:

Name: _____ Date: _____

$5\overline{)20}$ $7\overline{)56}$ $4\overline{)24}$ $7\overline{)63}$

$8\overline{)56}$ $3\overline{)15}$ $8\overline{)32}$ $4\overline{)40}$

$5\overline{)25}$ $9\overline{)63}$ $6\overline{)36}$ $7\overline{)21}$

$6\overline{)42}$ $6\overline{)30}$ $7\overline{)35}$ $5\overline{)15}$

$6\overline{)24}$ $9\overline{)36}$ $8\overline{)64}$ $3\overline{)27}$

Started: _____ Finished: _____ Total Time: _____ Completed: _____ Correct: _____

Name: _____ Date: _____

$56 \div 8 =$ $27 \div 3 =$

$49 \div 7 =$ $40 \div 5 =$

$6 \div 1 =$ $48 \div 6 =$

$32 \div 4 =$ $35 \div 7 =$

$30 \div 5 =$ $9 \div 3 =$

$36 \div 6 =$ $27 \div 9 =$

$24 \div 4 =$ $63 \div 7 =$

$72 \div 8 =$ $36 \div 4 =$

$48 \div 8 =$ $6 \div 2 =$

$63 \div 9 =$ $81 \div 9 =$

Started: Finished: Total Time: Completed: Correct:

Name: _____   Date: _____

$3\overline{)18}$ $4\overline{)36}$ $9\overline{)72}$ $7\overline{)63}$

$8\overline{)48}$ $6\overline{)48}$ $3\overline{)27}$ $1\overline{)4}$

$3\overline{)12}$ $9\overline{)63}$ $2\overline{)18}$ $6\overline{)36}$

$9\overline{)18}$ $6\overline{)24}$ $9\overline{)81}$ $4\overline{)12}$

$4\overline{)32}$ $8\overline{)56}$ $2\overline{)14}$ $3\overline{)21}$

Started: _____   Finished: _____   Total Time: _____   Completed: _____   Correct: _____

Name: _____   Date: _____

$24 \div 8 =$ $18 \div 2 =$ $15 \div 5 =$

$27 \div 3 =$ $36 \div 6 =$ $35 \div 5 =$

$36 \div 9 =$ $72 \div 8 =$ $63 \div 9 =$

$32 \div 8 =$ $48 \div 8 =$ $24 \div 4 =$

$8 \div 2 =$ $27 \div 9 =$ $18 \div 3 =$

$10 \div 2 =$ $21 \div 3 =$ $54 \div 6 =$

$30 \div 5 =$ $16 \div 4 =$ $15 \div 3 =$

$5 \div 1 =$ $35 \div 7 =$ $40 \div 8 =$

$12 \div 2 =$ $10 \div 5 =$ $28 \div 4 =$

$18 \div 6 =$ $49 \div 7 =$ $18 \div 9 =$

Started: Finished: Total Time: Completed: Correct:

Name: _____   Date: _____

$4\overline{)24}$ $6\overline{)18}$ $5\overline{)20}$ $9\overline{)27}$ $5\overline{)25}$

$1\overline{)6}$ $3\overline{)24}$ $9\overline{)72}$ $9\overline{)63}$ $4\overline{)32}$

$6\overline{)42}$ $5\overline{)40}$ $2\overline{)12}$ $4\overline{)36}$ $9\overline{)18}$

$3\overline{)12}$ $3\overline{)6}$ $4\overline{)20}$ $6\overline{)30}$ $5\overline{)30}$

$4\overline{)8}$ $6\overline{)12}$ $1\overline{)9}$ $5\overline{)35}$ $7\overline{)42}$

$7\overline{)14}$ $3\overline{)9}$ $7\overline{)35}$ $3\overline{)15}$ $8\overline{)64}$

Started: _____   Finished: _____   Total Time: _____   Completed: _____   Correct: _____

Name: _____   Date: _____

$3 \div 1 =$ $18 \div 6 =$ $25 \div 5 =$

$27 \div 9 =$ $12 \div 2 =$ $63 \div 9 =$

$9 \div 3 =$ $72 \div 8 =$ $30 \div 5 =$

$32 \div 4 =$ $16 \div 2 =$ $40 \div 5 =$

$18 \div 2 =$ $48 \div 8 =$ $18 \div 9 =$

$12 \div 4 =$ $24 \div 3 =$ $56 \div 8 =$

$30 \div 6 =$ $10 \div 5 =$ $63 \div 7 =$

$12 \div 6 =$ $35 \div 7 =$ $9 \div 1 =$

$20 \div 4 =$ $36 \div 4 =$ $28 \div 7 =$

$35 \div 5 =$ $15 \div 3 =$ $64 \div 8 =$

Started: Finished: Total Time: Completed: Correct:

Name: _____   Date: _____

$7\overline{)21}$ $6\overline{)30}$ $2\overline{)18}$ $9\overline{)36}$ $6\overline{)42}$

$6\overline{)24}$ $1\overline{)2}$ $5\overline{)45}$ $7\overline{)56}$ $5\overline{)20}$

$5\overline{)15}$ $8\overline{)32}$ $9\overline{)27}$ $3\overline{)12}$ $6\overline{)36}$

$4\overline{)28}$ $9\overline{)54}$ $7\overline{)42}$ $9\overline{)45}$ $6\overline{)48}$

$3\overline{)18}$ $5\overline{)5}$ $7\overline{)14}$ $2\overline{)10}$ $8\overline{)24}$

$4\overline{)24}$ $3\overline{)21}$ $9\overline{)81}$ $5\overline{)30}$ $8\overline{)48}$

Started: _____   Finished: _____   Total Time: _____   Completed: _____   Correct: _____

Name: _____   Date: _____

$21 \div 7 =$ $30 \div 6 =$ $16 \div 4 =$

$36 \div 9 =$ $42 \div 6 =$ $3 \div 1 =$

$18 \div 6 =$ $25 \div 5 =$ $27 \div 9 =$

$12 \div 2 =$ $18 \div 9 =$ $12 \div 6 =$

$20 \div 5 =$ $24 \div 4 =$ $24 \div 8 =$

$6 \div 2 =$ $18 \div 2 =$ $15 \div 5 =$

$27 \div 3 =$ $36 \div 6 =$ $18 \div 3 =$

$36 \div 4 =$ $72 \div 9 =$ $63 \div 7 =$

$48 \div 8 =$ $54 \div 9 =$ $48 \div 6 =$

$56 \div 7 =$ $4 \div 2 =$ $15 \div 3 =$

Started: Finished: Total Time: Completed: Correct:

Name: _____   Date: _____

$6\overline{)24}$ $1\overline{)2}$ $5\overline{)45}$ $7\overline{)56}$ $5\overline{)20}$

$4\overline{)36}$ $7\overline{)28}$ $7\overline{)35}$ $3\overline{)15}$ $8\overline{)64}$

$1\overline{)6}$ $3\overline{)24}$ $9\overline{)72}$ $9\overline{)63}$ $4\overline{)32}$

$5\overline{)35}$ $9\overline{)36}$ $8\overline{)72}$ $7\overline{)63}$ $8\overline{)32}$

$6\overline{)48}$ $3\overline{)27}$ $1\overline{)4}$ $9\overline{)81}$ $4\overline{)12}$

$3\overline{)12}$ $9\overline{)18}$ $2\overline{)18}$ $6\overline{)36}$ $6\overline{)54}$

$2\overline{)10}$ $8\overline{)48}$ $5\overline{)25}$ $8\overline{)16}$ $2\overline{)14}$

$7\overline{)49}$ $4\overline{)20}$ $6\overline{)12}$ $2\overline{)6}$ $3\overline{)18}$

Started: _____   Finished: _____   Total Time: _____   Completed: _____   Correct: _____

Name: _____   Date: _____

$8 \div 4 =$	$9 \div 9 =$	$16 \div 4 =$	$30 \div 6 =$	$54 \div 6 =$
$42 \div 6 =$	$40 \div 5 =$	$12 \div 2 =$	$36 \div 4 =$	$18 \div 9 =$
$15 \div 5 =$	$32 \div 8 =$	$27 \div 9 =$	$12 \div 3 =$	$36 \div 6 =$
$40 \div 8 =$	$42 \div 7 =$	$64 \div 8 =$	$45 \div 9 =$	$21 \div 7 =$
$14 \div 7 =$	$24 \div 8 =$	$18 \div 6 =$	$18 \div 3 =$	$7 \div 1 =$
$54 \div 9 =$	$9 \div 3 =$	$72 \div 9 =$	$30 \div 5 =$	$28 \div 4 =$
$56 \div 8 =$	$24 \div 4 =$	$8 \div 2 =$	$63 \div 9 =$	$21 \div 3 =$
$36 \div 9 =$	$32 \div 4 =$	$72 \div 8 =$	$16 \div 2 =$	$6 \div 3 =$

Started: _____   Finished: _____   Total Time: _____   Completed: _____   Correct: _____

Name: _____   Date: _____

$5\overline{)20}$ $2\overline{)16}$ $5\overline{)40}$ $2\overline{)18}$ $8\overline{)48}$

$9\overline{)18}$ $1\overline{)3}$ $6\overline{)18}$ $3\overline{)27}$ $5\overline{)10}$

$6\overline{)42}$ $5\overline{)30}$ $7\overline{)56}$ $9\overline{)81}$ $4\overline{)12}$

$3\overline{)12}$ $7\overline{)63}$ $3\overline{)6}$ $5\overline{)35}$ $4\overline{)20}$

$2\overline{)8}$ $2\overline{)10}$ $6\overline{)48}$ $3\overline{)21}$ $6\overline{)54}$

$5\overline{)15}$ $7\overline{)49}$ $6\overline{)30}$ $3\overline{)15}$ $8\overline{)32}$

$9\overline{)72}$ $2\overline{)4}$ $7\overline{)42}$ $8\overline{)16}$ $4\overline{)16}$

$9\overline{)45}$ $2\overline{)14}$ $7\overline{)28}$ $5\overline{)45}$ $1\overline{)8}$

Started: _____   Finished: _____   Total Time: _____   Completed: _____   Correct: _____

Name: _____   Date: _____

$8 \div 2 =$ $12 \div 6 =$ $9 \div 1 =$ $35 \div 5 =$ $42 \div 7 =$

$14 \div 7 =$ $10 \div 2 =$ $24 \div 3 =$ $24 \div 4 =$ $25 \div 5 =$

$63 \div 7 =$ $6 \div 6 =$ $36 \div 6 =$ $7 \div 1 =$ $20 \div 4 =$

$15 \div 3 =$ $5 \div 1 =$ $21 \div 7 =$ $48 \div 6 =$ $36 \div 9 =$

$54 \div 6 =$ $16 \div 8 =$ $9 \div 9 =$ $24 \div 6 =$ $56 \div 7 =$

$12 \div 4 =$ $27 \div 9 =$ $30 \div 5 =$ $21 \div 3 =$ $18 \div 6 =$

$30 \div 6 =$ $24 \div 8 =$ $28 \div 4 =$ $48 \div 8 =$ $36 \div 4 =$

$40 \div 8 =$ $12 \div 2 =$ $18 \div 3 =$ $5 \div 5 =$ $81 \div 9 =$

Started: Finished: Total Time: Completed: Correct:

Name: _____   Date: _____

$2\overline{)6}$ $3\overline{)12}$ $6\overline{)24}$ $8\overline{)32}$ $9\overline{)63}$

$7\overline{)14}$ $3\overline{)9}$ $7\overline{)35}$ $1\overline{)8}$ $5\overline{)15}$

$3\overline{)15}$ $8\overline{)64}$ $2\overline{)12}$ $8\overline{)40}$ $4\overline{)20}$

$4\overline{)24}$ $3\overline{)21}$ $9\overline{)81}$ $5\overline{)30}$ $6\overline{)42}$

$5\overline{)25}$ $7\overline{)21}$ $5\overline{)45}$ $8\overline{)72}$ $9\overline{)27}$

$7\overline{)7}$ $9\overline{)36}$ $5\overline{)40}$ $7\overline{)63}$ $2\overline{)14}$

$4\overline{)16}$ $2\overline{)8}$ $3\overline{)24}$ $3\overline{)18}$ $5\overline{)35}$

$4\overline{)28}$ $9\overline{)54}$ $7\overline{)42}$ $9\overline{)45}$ $6\overline{)48}$

$5\overline{)10}$ $4\overline{)8}$ $6\overline{)18}$ $9\overline{)18}$ $8\overline{)56}$

$3\overline{)27}$ $5\overline{)20}$ $8\overline{)24}$ $7\overline{)49}$ $2\overline{)16}$

Started: _____ Finished: _____ Total Time: _____ Completed: _____ Correct: _____

Name: _____   Date: _____

$9 \div 3 =$ $12 \div 4 =$ $24 \div 6 =$ $64 \div 8 =$ $49 \div 7 =$

$30 \div 6 =$ $1 \div 1 =$ $16 \div 4 =$ $14 \div 2 =$ $48 \div 8 =$

$28 \div 7 =$ $36 \div 6 =$ $48 \div 6 =$ $5 \div 1 =$ $20 \div 5 =$

$72 \div 8 =$ $21 \div 3 =$ $7 \div 1 =$ $54 \div 6 =$ $16 \div 2 =$

$2 \div 2 =$ $27 \div 3 =$ $36 \div 4 =$ $63 \div 7 =$ $8 \div 2 =$

$18 \div 2 =$ $5 \div 5 =$ $32 \div 8 =$ $18 \div 3 =$ $9 \div 1 =$

$8 \div 8 =$ $18 \div 9 =$ $10 \div 2 =$ $42 \div 7 =$ $45 \div 9 =$

$12 \div 3 =$ $72 \div 9 =$ $24 \div 4 =$ $35 \div 5 =$ $42 \div 6 =$

$24 \div 3 =$ $8 \div 4 =$ $16 \div 8 =$ $15 \div 3 =$ $45 \div 5 =$

$14 \div 7 =$ $12 \div 2 =$ $24 \div 8 =$ $20 \div 4 =$ $25 \div 5 =$

Started: Finished: Total Time: Completed: Correct:

Name: _____   Date: _____

$3\overline{)12}$ $4\overline{)24}$ $6\overline{)36}$ $8\overline{)40}$ $3\overline{)21}$

$9\overline{)27}$ $4\overline{)28}$ $1\overline{)2}$ $5\overline{)10}$ $7\overline{)7}$

$2\overline{)18}$ $3\overline{)3}$ $6\overline{)12}$ $8\overline{)56}$ $8\overline{)72}$

$6\overline{)48}$ $9\overline{)36}$ $5\overline{)30}$ $1\overline{)6}$ $4\overline{)20}$

$4\overline{)12}$ $8\overline{)16}$ $2\overline{)6}$ $6\overline{)30}$ $4\overline{)32}$

$8\overline{)8}$ $6\overline{)18}$ $2\overline{)10}$ $7\overline{)42}$ $9\overline{)45}$

$8\overline{)32}$ $7\overline{)21}$ $3\overline{)15}$ $6\overline{)54}$ $5\overline{)35}$

$5\overline{)45}$ $8\overline{)64}$ $2\overline{)16}$ $6\overline{)24}$ $1\overline{)8}$

$9\overline{)18}$ $4\overline{)8}$ $3\overline{)24}$ $6\overline{)42}$ $9\overline{)54}$

$2\overline{)8}$ $6\overline{)6}$ $8\overline{)48}$ $7\overline{)56}$ $3\overline{)18}$

Started: Finished: Total Time: Completed: Correct:

Name: _____   Date: _____

$6 \div 3 =$	$30 \div 5 =$	$48 \div 6 =$	$27 \div 9 =$	$28 \div 4 =$
$25 \div 5 =$	$21 \div 7 =$	$16 \div 8 =$	$40 \div 8 =$	$4 \div 4 =$
$24 \div 3 =$	$18 \div 2 =$	$56 \div 7 =$	$15 \div 5 =$	$48 \div 8 =$
$81 \div 9 =$	$14 \div 7 =$	$12 \div 4 =$	$36 \div 4 =$	$3 \div 1 =$
$24 \div 4 =$	$63 \div 9 =$	$21 \div 3 =$	$9 \div 3 =$	$16 \div 2 =$
$4 \div 1 =$	$15 \div 3 =$	$24 \div 6 =$	$45 \div 9 =$	$35 \div 5 =$
$20 \div 4 =$	$24 \div 8 =$	$36 \div 6 =$	$30 \div 6 =$	$32 \div 8 =$
$35 \div 7 =$	$40 \div 5 =$	$56 \div 8 =$	$9 \div 9 =$	$12 \div 2 =$
$42 \div 6 =$	$12 \div 6 =$	$18 \div 6 =$	$7 \div 1 =$	$42 \div 7 =$
$54 \div 9 =$	$6 \div 2 =$	$49 \div 7 =$	$32 \div 4 =$	$72 \div 8 =$

Started: _____   Finished: _____   Total Time: _____   Completed: _____   Correct: _____

Name: _____   Date: _____

$10\overline{)30}$ $11\overline{)66}$ $12\overline{)48}$ $10\overline{)60}$

$10\overline{)50}$ $12\overline{)60}$ $11\overline{)33}$ $10\overline{)40}$

$10\overline{)70}$ $11\overline{)55}$ $10\overline{)80}$ $11\overline{)88}$

$10\overline{)90}$ $11\overline{)77}$ $12\overline{)24}$ $10\overline{)100}$

$11\overline{)22}$ $10\overline{)20}$ $12\overline{)36}$ $10\overline{)120}$

Started: Finished: Total Time: Completed: Correct:

Name: _____

Date: _____

$11 \div 11 =$

$48 \div 12 =$

$60 \div 10 =$

$132 \div 11 =$

$22 \div 11 =$

$50 \div 10 =$

$77 \div 11 =$

$72 \div 12 =$

$70 \div 10 =$

$33 \div 11 =$

$84 \div 12 =$

$88 \div 11 =$

$44 \div 11 =$

$24 \div 12 =$

$99 \div 11 =$

$30 \div 10 =$

$60 \div 12 =$

$121 \div 11 =$

$40 \div 10 =$

$144 \div 12 =$

Started: _____ Finished: _____ Total Time: _____ Completed: _____ Correct: _____

Name: _____   Date: _____

$12\overline{)36}$ $11\overline{)22}$ $12\overline{)84}$ $12\overline{)132}$

$10\overline{)50}$ $12\overline{)60}$ $11\overline{)44}$ $12\overline{)108}$

$11\overline{)66}$ $12\overline{)72}$ $11\overline{)55}$ $12\overline{)120}$

$12\overline{)24}$ $10\overline{)60}$ $12\overline{)96}$ $11\overline{)88}$

$12\overline{)12}$ $10\overline{)90}$ $12\overline{)48}$ $12\overline{)144}$

Started: Finished: Total Time: Completed: Correct:

20

Name: _____   Date: _____

$$\begin{array}{r} 6 \\ +\ 1 \\ \hline \end{array}$$

$$\begin{array}{r} 3 \\ \times\ 3 \\ \hline \end{array}$$

$$\begin{array}{r} 4 \\ -\ 4 \\ \hline \end{array}$$

$$25 \div 5 =$$

$$\begin{array}{r} 3 \\ \times\ 7 \\ \hline \end{array}$$

$$\begin{array}{r} 15 \\ -\ 6 \\ \hline \end{array}$$

$$42 \div 6 =$$

$$\begin{array}{r} 6 \\ +\ 2 \\ \hline \end{array}$$

$$\begin{array}{r} 4 \\ +\ 9 \\ \hline \end{array}$$

$$72 \div 8 =$$

$$\begin{array}{r} 16 \\ -\ 7 \\ \hline \end{array}$$

$$\begin{array}{r} 8 \\ \times\ 4 \\ \hline \end{array}$$

$$18 \div 6 =$$

$$\begin{array}{r} 5 \\ \times\ 2 \\ \hline \end{array}$$

$$\begin{array}{r} 8 \\ \times\ 6 \\ \hline \end{array}$$

$$\begin{array}{r} 7 \\ -\ 3 \\ \hline \end{array}$$

$$\begin{array}{r} 6 \\ +\ 4 \\ \hline \end{array}$$

$$\begin{array}{r} 12 \\ -\ 6 \\ \hline \end{array}$$

$$48 \div 8 =$$

$$\begin{array}{r} 4 \\ \times\ 9 \\ \hline \end{array}$$

Started: _____   Finished: _____   Total Time: _____   Completed: _____   Correct: _____

Name: _____ Date: _____

$$\begin{array}{r} 4 \\ +6 \\ \hline \end{array} \qquad \begin{array}{r} 16 \\ -8 \\ \hline \end{array} \qquad 4\overline{)32} \qquad \begin{array}{r} 5 \\ \times 8 \\ \hline \end{array}$$

$$\begin{array}{r} 7 \\ +2 \\ \hline \end{array} \qquad \begin{array}{r} 6 \\ \times 4 \\ \hline \end{array} \qquad \begin{array}{r} 10 \\ -7 \\ \hline \end{array} \qquad 7\overline{)49}$$

$$\begin{array}{r} 6 \\ \times 2 \\ \hline \end{array} \qquad \begin{array}{r} 18 \\ -9 \\ \hline \end{array} \qquad 5\overline{)45} \qquad \begin{array}{r} 9 \\ +1 \\ \hline \end{array}$$

$$\begin{array}{r} 5 \\ +8 \\ \hline \end{array} \qquad 7\overline{)21} \qquad \begin{array}{r} 13 \\ -4 \\ \hline \end{array} \qquad \begin{array}{r} 8 \\ \times 3 \\ \hline \end{array}$$

$$3\overline{)27} \qquad \begin{array}{r} 9 \\ \times 3 \\ \hline \end{array} \qquad \begin{array}{r} 8 \\ \times 7 \\ \hline \end{array} \qquad \begin{array}{r} 5 \\ +5 \\ \hline \end{array}$$

Started: _____ Finished: _____ Total Time: _____ Completed: _____ Correct: _____

Name: _____   Date: _____

$$\begin{array}{r} 4 \\ + 5 \\ \hline \end{array}$$
$$\begin{array}{r} 10 \\ - 3 \\ \hline \end{array}$$
$$\begin{array}{r} 2 \\ \times 3 \\ \hline \end{array}$$
$$30 \div 6 =$$

$$\begin{array}{r} 12 \\ - 8 \\ \hline \end{array}$$
$$\begin{array}{r} 8 \\ + 8 \\ \hline \end{array}$$
$$24 \div 2 =$$
$$\begin{array}{r} 8 \\ \times 2 \\ \hline \end{array}$$

$$\begin{array}{r} 6 \\ + 6 \\ \hline \end{array}$$
$$36 \div 4 =$$
$$\begin{array}{r} 13 \\ - 6 \\ \hline \end{array}$$
$$\begin{array}{r} 6 \\ \times 5 \\ \hline \end{array}$$

$$48 \div 8 =$$
$$\begin{array}{r} 9 \\ + 3 \\ \hline \end{array}$$
$$\begin{array}{r} 5 \\ \times 2 \\ \hline \end{array}$$
$$\begin{array}{r} 18 \\ - 9 \\ \hline \end{array}$$

$$\begin{array}{r} 9 \\ \times 6 \\ \hline \end{array}$$
$$\begin{array}{r} 14 \\ - 7 \\ \hline \end{array}$$
$$56 \div 7 =$$
$$\begin{array}{r} 9 \\ + 2 \\ \hline \end{array}$$

Started: Finished: Total Time: Completed: Correct:

Name: _____   Date: _____

$$3\overline{)18} \qquad \begin{array}{r} 7 \\ \times 4 \\ \hline \end{array} \qquad \begin{array}{r} 9 \\ -3 \\ \hline \end{array} \qquad \begin{array}{r} 8 \\ +6 \\ \hline \end{array}$$

$$\begin{array}{r} 5 \\ +4 \\ \hline \end{array} \qquad 8\overline{)24} \qquad \begin{array}{r} 3 \\ \times 4 \\ \hline \end{array} \qquad \begin{array}{r} 7 \\ -7 \\ \hline \end{array}$$

$$\begin{array}{r} 3 \\ \times 7 \\ \hline \end{array} \qquad \begin{array}{r} 17 \\ -9 \\ \hline \end{array} \qquad 7\overline{)28} \qquad \begin{array}{r} 5 \\ +7 \\ \hline \end{array}$$

$$\begin{array}{r} 5 \\ +8 \\ \hline \end{array} \qquad 7\overline{)21} \qquad \begin{array}{r} 13 \\ -4 \\ \hline \end{array} \qquad \begin{array}{r} 8 \\ \times 3 \\ \hline \end{array}$$

$$3\overline{)12} \qquad \begin{array}{r} 9 \\ \times 3 \\ \hline \end{array} \qquad \begin{array}{r} 8 \\ +7 \\ \hline \end{array} \qquad \begin{array}{r} 5 \\ -5 \\ \hline \end{array}$$

Started: _____ Finished: _____ Total Time: _____ Completed: _____ Correct: _____

Name: _____ Date: _____

$$6 \times 7$$

$$4 + 4$$

$$9 - 3$$

$$18 \div 2 =$$

$$8 + 3$$

$$9 - 5$$

$$36 \div 6 =$$

$$6 \times 6$$

$$15 \div 3 =$$

$$8 \times 6$$

$$6 - 5$$

$$5 + 3$$

$$6 + 5$$

$$9 \times 9$$

$$9 - 7$$

$$72 \div 8 =$$

$$5 + 4$$

$$8 - 7$$

$$9 \times 6$$

$$42 \div 6 =$$

Started: _____ Finished: _____ Total Time: _____ Completed: _____ Correct: _____

Name: _____   Date: _____

$$\begin{array}{r} 8 \\ + 6 \\ \hline \end{array}$$
$$\begin{array}{r} 8 \\ - 4 \\ \hline \end{array}$$
$$9\overline{)54}$$
$$\begin{array}{r} 5 \\ \times 7 \\ \hline \end{array}$$
$$\begin{array}{r} 5 \\ + 3 \\ \hline \end{array}$$

$$6\overline{)30}$$
$$\begin{array}{r} 8 \\ \times 5 \\ \hline \end{array}$$
$$\begin{array}{r} 15 \\ - 7 \\ \hline \end{array}$$
$$\begin{array}{r} 8 \\ - 2 \\ \hline \end{array}$$
$$5\overline{)20}$$

$$\begin{array}{r} 9 \\ \times 9 \\ \hline \end{array}$$
$$\begin{array}{r} 7 \\ + 4 \\ \hline \end{array}$$
$$\begin{array}{r} 6 \\ - 4 \\ \hline \end{array}$$
$$4\overline{)28}$$
$$\begin{array}{r} 5 \\ \times 9 \\ \hline \end{array}$$

$$\begin{array}{r} 5 \\ \times 5 \\ \hline \end{array}$$
$$\begin{array}{r} 7 \\ + 6 \\ \hline \end{array}$$
$$\begin{array}{r} 12 \\ - 8 \\ \hline \end{array}$$
$$8\overline{)40}$$
$$\begin{array}{r} 9 \\ + 7 \\ \hline \end{array}$$

$$\begin{array}{r} 4 \\ + 9 \\ \hline \end{array}$$
$$\begin{array}{r} 9 \\ - 6 \\ \hline \end{array}$$
$$6\overline{)54}$$
$$\begin{array}{r} 6 \\ \times 8 \\ \hline \end{array}$$
$$5\overline{)40}$$

$$6\overline{)24}$$
$$\begin{array}{r} 5 \\ \times 6 \\ \hline \end{array}$$
$$\begin{array}{r} 7 \\ - 5 \\ \hline \end{array}$$
$$\begin{array}{r} 8 \\ + 4 \\ \hline \end{array}$$
$$\begin{array}{r} 15 \\ - 8 \\ \hline \end{array}$$

Started: _____ Finished: _____ Total Time: _____ Completed: _____ Correct: _____

Name: _____ Date: _____

$$\begin{array}{r} 4 \\ \times 5 \\ \hline \end{array}$$ $$\begin{array}{r} 5 \\ + 8 \\ \hline \end{array}$$ $$\begin{array}{r} 14 \\ - 5 \\ \hline \end{array}$$ $32 \div 8 =$ $$\begin{array}{r} 9 \\ + 9 \\ \hline \end{array}$$

$$\begin{array}{r} 7 \\ + 8 \\ \hline \end{array}$$ $$\begin{array}{r} 7 \\ - 6 \\ \hline \end{array}$$ $63 \div 7 =$ $$\begin{array}{r} 8 \\ \times 8 \\ \hline \end{array}$$ $$\begin{array}{r} 15 \\ - 9 \\ \hline \end{array}$$

$35 \div 5 =$ $$\begin{array}{r} 9 \\ \times 7 \\ \hline \end{array}$$ $$\begin{array}{r} 10 \\ - 5 \\ \hline \end{array}$$ $$\begin{array}{r} 8 \\ + 4 \\ \hline \end{array}$$ $$\begin{array}{r} 6 \\ \times 6 \\ \hline \end{array}$$

$$\begin{array}{r} 7 \\ \times 7 \\ \hline \end{array}$$ $27 \div 3 =$ $$\begin{array}{r} 9 \\ \times 5 \\ \hline \end{array}$$ $$\begin{array}{r} 7 \\ - 3 \\ \hline \end{array}$$ $$\begin{array}{r} 9 \\ + 6 \\ \hline \end{array}$$

$$\begin{array}{r} 9 \\ + 5 \\ \hline \end{array}$$ $$\begin{array}{r} 3 \\ \times 8 \\ \hline \end{array}$$ $$\begin{array}{r} 6 \\ + 5 \\ \hline \end{array}$$ $$\begin{array}{r} 7 \\ + 7 \\ \hline \end{array}$$ $28 \div 4 =$

$48 \div 6 =$ $$\begin{array}{r} 9 \\ \times 9 \\ \hline \end{array}$$ $$\begin{array}{r} 7 \\ + 4 \\ \hline \end{array}$$ $$\begin{array}{r} 6 \\ - 4 \\ \hline \end{array}$$ $$\begin{array}{r} 7 \\ + 9 \\ \hline \end{array}$$

Started: Finished: Total Time: Completed: Correct:

Name: _____   Date: _____

$$\begin{array}{r} 12 \\ -\ 7 \\ \hline \end{array} \qquad \begin{array}{r} 9 \\ +\ 8 \\ \hline \end{array} \qquad 2\overline{)18} \qquad \begin{array}{r} 8 \\ \times\ 2 \\ \hline \end{array} \qquad \begin{array}{r} 9 \\ -\ 4 \\ \hline \end{array}$$

$$\begin{array}{r} 3 \\ +\ 6 \\ \hline \end{array} \qquad \begin{array}{r} 14 \\ -\ 9 \\ \hline \end{array} \qquad \begin{array}{r} 7 \\ +\ 5 \\ \hline \end{array} \qquad 7\overline{)35} \qquad \begin{array}{r} 8 \\ \times\ 9 \\ \hline \end{array}$$

$$6\overline{)48} \qquad \begin{array}{r} 3 \\ \times\ 6 \\ \hline \end{array} \qquad \begin{array}{r} 17 \\ -\ 8 \\ \hline \end{array} \qquad \begin{array}{r} 3 \\ +\ 4 \\ \hline \end{array} \qquad \begin{array}{r} 11 \\ -\ 6 \\ \hline \end{array}$$

$$\begin{array}{r} 7 \\ \times\ 5 \\ \hline \end{array} \qquad \begin{array}{r} 1 \\ +\ 6 \\ \hline \end{array} \qquad \begin{array}{r} 12 \\ -\ 5 \\ \hline \end{array} \qquad 8\overline{)16} \qquad \begin{array}{r} 7 \\ \times\ 2 \\ \hline \end{array}$$

$$\begin{array}{r} 6 \\ +\ 9 \\ \hline \end{array} \qquad \begin{array}{r} 10 \\ -\ 4 \\ \hline \end{array} \qquad 7\overline{)56} \qquad \begin{array}{r} 4 \\ \times\ 9 \\ \hline \end{array} \qquad \begin{array}{r} 5 \\ +\ 5 \\ \hline \end{array}$$

$$\begin{array}{r} 15 \\ -\ 8 \\ \hline \end{array} \qquad \begin{array}{r} 4 \\ +\ 7 \\ \hline \end{array} \qquad 2\overline{)14} \qquad \begin{array}{r} 9 \\ \times\ 2 \\ \hline \end{array} \qquad \begin{array}{r} 6 \\ +\ 3 \\ \hline \end{array}$$

Started: _____   Finished: _____   Total Time: _____   Completed: _____   Correct: _____

Name: _____ Date: _____

$$\begin{array}{r} 8 \\ +2 \end{array}$$
$$\begin{array}{r} 6 \\ -3 \end{array}$$
$18 \div 6 =$
$$\begin{array}{r} 6 \\ \times 4 \end{array}$$
$$\begin{array}{r} 7 \\ \times 8 \end{array}$$

$56 \div 8 =$
$$\begin{array}{r} 7 \\ \times 6 \end{array}$$
$$\begin{array}{r} 15 \\ -7 \end{array}$$
$$\begin{array}{r} 7 \\ +3 \end{array}$$
$$\begin{array}{r} 8 \\ -2 \end{array}$$

$$\begin{array}{r} 8 \\ +4 \end{array}$$
$$\begin{array}{r} 6 \\ +6 \end{array}$$
$$\begin{array}{r} 12 \\ -9 \end{array}$$
$$\begin{array}{r} 10 \\ \times 8 \end{array}$$
$40 \div 8 =$

$$\begin{array}{r} 6 \\ \times 5 \end{array}$$
$$\begin{array}{r} 9 \\ +4 \end{array}$$
$48 \div 4 =$
$$\begin{array}{r} 10 \\ -7 \end{array}$$
$$\begin{array}{r} 9 \\ +7 \end{array}$$

$54 \div 6 =$
$$\begin{array}{r} 10 \\ -8 \end{array}$$
$$\begin{array}{r} 8 \\ +9 \end{array}$$
$$\begin{array}{r} 12 \\ -5 \end{array}$$
$$\begin{array}{r} 7 \\ \times 7 \end{array}$$

$$\begin{array}{r} 16 \\ -8 \end{array}$$
$28 \div 4 =$
$$\begin{array}{r} 8 \\ \times 5 \end{array}$$
$$\begin{array}{r} 5 \\ +9 \end{array}$$
$$\begin{array}{r} 17 \\ -8 \end{array}$$

Started: _____ Finished: _____ Total Time: _____ Completed: _____ Correct: _____

30

Name: _____   Date: _____

$9\overline{)81}$ $\begin{array}{r} 7 \\ +5 \\ \hline \end{array}$ $\begin{array}{r} 10 \\ -5 \\ \hline \end{array}$ $\begin{array}{r} 12 \\ \times 3 \\ \hline \end{array}$ $6\overline{)30}$

$\begin{array}{r} 12 \\ -8 \\ \hline \end{array}$ $\begin{array}{r} 8 \\ +8 \\ \hline \end{array}$ $2\overline{)24}$ $\begin{array}{r} 7 \\ \times 2 \\ \hline \end{array}$ $\begin{array}{r} 9 \\ +9 \\ \hline \end{array}$

$\begin{array}{r} 6 \\ \times 4 \\ \hline \end{array}$ $\begin{array}{r} 7 \\ +6 \\ \hline \end{array}$ $4\overline{)36}$ $\begin{array}{r} 16 \\ -9 \\ \hline \end{array}$ $\begin{array}{r} 6 \\ \times 5 \\ \hline \end{array}$

$8\overline{)48}$ $\begin{array}{r} 15 \\ -7 \\ \hline \end{array}$ $\begin{array}{r} 9 \\ +3 \\ \hline \end{array}$ $\begin{array}{r} 5 \\ \times 4 \\ \hline \end{array}$ $\begin{array}{r} 18 \\ -9 \\ \hline \end{array}$

$\begin{array}{r} 9 \\ \times 6 \\ \hline \end{array}$ $\begin{array}{r} 14 \\ -7 \\ \hline \end{array}$ $8\overline{)56}$ $\begin{array}{r} 9 \\ +4 \\ \hline \end{array}$ $\begin{array}{r} 8 \\ \times 7 \\ \hline \end{array}$

$\begin{array}{r} 7 \\ +4 \\ \hline \end{array}$ $\begin{array}{r} 6 \\ -5 \\ \hline \end{array}$ $\begin{array}{r} 7 \\ \times 3 \\ \hline \end{array}$ $7\overline{)35}$ $\begin{array}{r} 9 \\ +7 \\ \hline \end{array}$

Started: _____   Finished: _____   Total Time: _____   Completed: _____   Correct: _____

Name: _____ Date: _____

$$\begin{array}{r} 7 \\ + 3 \\ \hline \end{array}$$
$$\begin{array}{r} 16 \\ - 8 \\ \hline \end{array}$$
$$\begin{array}{r} 6 \\ \times 8 \\ \hline \end{array}$$
$$\begin{array}{r} 5 \\ + 6 \\ \hline \end{array}$$
$$21 \div 7 =$$

$$\begin{array}{r} 8 \\ + 2 \\ \hline \end{array}$$
$$\begin{array}{r} 6 \\ \times 7 \\ \hline \end{array}$$
$$18 \div 2 =$$
$$\begin{array}{r} 4 \\ + 4 \\ \hline \end{array}$$
$$\begin{array}{r} 9 \\ - 3 \\ \hline \end{array}$$

$$\begin{array}{r} 6 \\ - 3 \\ \hline \end{array}$$
$$\begin{array}{r} 8 \\ + 3 \\ \hline \end{array}$$
$$\begin{array}{r} 9 \\ - 5 \\ \hline \end{array}$$
$$36 \div 4 =$$
$$\begin{array}{r} 6 \\ \times 6 \\ \hline \end{array}$$

$$15 \div 5 =$$
$$\begin{array}{r} 8 \\ \times 6 \\ \hline \end{array}$$
$$\begin{array}{r} 14 \\ - 5 \\ \hline \end{array}$$
$$\begin{array}{r} 5 \\ + 3 \\ \hline \end{array}$$
$$12 \div 4 =$$

$$\begin{array}{r} 6 \\ \times 4 \\ \hline \end{array}$$
$$72 \div 8 =$$
$$\begin{array}{r} 6 \\ + 5 \\ \hline \end{array}$$
$$81 \div 9 =$$
$$\begin{array}{r} 9 \\ - 7 \\ \hline \end{array}$$

$$\begin{array}{r} 5 \\ + 4 \\ \hline \end{array}$$
$$\begin{array}{r} 8 \\ - 7 \\ \hline \end{array}$$
$$\begin{array}{r} 9 \\ \times 6 \\ \hline \end{array}$$
$$42 \div 7 =$$
$$\begin{array}{r} 9 \\ \times 8 \\ \hline \end{array}$$

$$64 \div 8 =$$
$$\begin{array}{r} 7 \\ \times 6 \\ \hline \end{array}$$
$$\begin{array}{r} 15 \\ - 7 \\ \hline \end{array}$$
$$\begin{array}{r} 7 \\ + 4 \\ \hline \end{array}$$
$$\begin{array}{r} 8 \\ - 2 \\ \hline \end{array}$$

$$\begin{array}{r} 4 \\ \times 4 \\ \hline \end{array}$$
$$\begin{array}{r} 6 \\ - 0 \\ \hline \end{array}$$
$$\begin{array}{r} 7 \\ \times 3 \\ \hline \end{array}$$
$$54 \div 6 =$$
$$\begin{array}{r} 5 \\ + 9 \\ \hline \end{array}$$

Started: _____ Finished: _____ Total Time: _____ Completed: _____ Correct: _____

Name: _____   Date: _____

$$
\begin{array}{r} 4 \\ +9 \\ \hline \end{array}
\qquad
\begin{array}{r} 9 \\ -6 \\ \hline \end{array}
\qquad
6\overline{)54}
\qquad
\begin{array}{r} 6 \\ \times 8 \\ \hline \end{array}
\qquad
5\overline{)40}
$$

$$
\begin{array}{r} 3 \\ \times 6 \\ \hline \end{array}
\qquad
\begin{array}{r} 9 \\ +7 \\ \hline \end{array}
\qquad
7\overline{)21}
\qquad
\begin{array}{r} 9 \\ \times 9 \\ \hline \end{array}
\qquad
\begin{array}{r} 5 \\ +7 \\ \hline \end{array}
$$

$$
\begin{array}{r} 16 \\ -7 \\ \hline \end{array}
\qquad
3\overline{)18}
\qquad
\begin{array}{r} 7 \\ \times 4 \\ \hline \end{array}
\qquad
\begin{array}{r} 9 \\ \times 3 \\ \hline \end{array}
\qquad
\begin{array}{r} 8 \\ +6 \\ \hline \end{array}
$$

$$
7\overline{)42}
\qquad
\begin{array}{r} 5 \\ +8 \\ \hline \end{array}
\qquad
\begin{array}{r} 5 \\ +3 \\ \hline \end{array}
\qquad
\begin{array}{r} 13 \\ -4 \\ \hline \end{array}
\qquad
\begin{array}{r} 8 \\ \times 3 \\ \hline \end{array}
$$

$$
6\overline{)36}
\qquad
\begin{array}{r} 5 \\ +4 \\ \hline \end{array}
\qquad
8\overline{)24}
\qquad
\begin{array}{r} 3 \\ \times 4 \\ \hline \end{array}
\qquad
\begin{array}{r} 7 \\ -7 \\ \hline \end{array}
$$

$$
\begin{array}{r} 3 \\ \times 7 \\ \hline \end{array}
\qquad
5\overline{)15}
\qquad
\begin{array}{r} 17 \\ -9 \\ \hline \end{array}
\qquad
7\overline{)28}
\qquad
\begin{array}{r} 8 \\ +7 \\ \hline \end{array}
$$

$$
6\overline{)24}
\qquad
\begin{array}{r} 5 \\ \times 6 \\ \hline \end{array}
\qquad
\begin{array}{r} 7 \\ -5 \\ \hline \end{array}
\qquad
\begin{array}{r} 7 \\ +4 \\ \hline \end{array}
\qquad
\begin{array}{r} 15 \\ -8 \\ \hline \end{array}
$$

$$
3\overline{)12}
\qquad
\begin{array}{r} 7 \\ \times 3 \\ \hline \end{array}
\qquad
\begin{array}{r} 7 \\ +8 \\ \hline \end{array}
\qquad
2\overline{)6}
\qquad
\begin{array}{r} 5 \\ -5 \\ \hline \end{array}
$$

Started: Finished: Total Time: Completed: Correct:

Name: _____   Date: _____

$$\begin{array}{r} 8 \\ -3 \\ \hline \end{array}$$ $$\begin{array}{r} 4 \\ +6 \\ \hline \end{array}$$ $$\begin{array}{r} 16 \\ -8 \\ \hline \end{array}$$ $32 \div 8 =$ $$\begin{array}{r} 5 \\ \times 8 \\ \hline \end{array}$$

$49 \div 7 =$ $$\begin{array}{r} 7 \\ +2 \\ \hline \end{array}$$ $$\begin{array}{r} 6 \\ \times 4 \\ \hline \end{array}$$ $$\begin{array}{r} 10 \\ -7 \\ \hline \end{array}$$ $$\begin{array}{r} 3 \\ \times 3 \\ \hline \end{array}$$

$$\begin{array}{r} 6 \\ \times 7 \\ \hline \end{array}$$ $$\begin{array}{r} 6 \\ \times 2 \\ \hline \end{array}$$ $$\begin{array}{r} 18 \\ -9 \\ \hline \end{array}$$ $$\begin{array}{r} 9 \\ +0 \\ \hline \end{array}$$ $45 \div 5 =$

$$\begin{array}{r} 7 \\ -3 \\ \hline \end{array}$$ $$\begin{array}{r} 9 \\ \times 4 \\ \hline \end{array}$$ $$\begin{array}{r} 6 \\ +7 \\ \hline \end{array}$$ $30 \div 6 =$ $$\begin{array}{r} 8 \\ -4 \\ \hline \end{array}$$

$42 \div 6 =$ $$\begin{array}{r} 6 \\ +8 \\ \hline \end{array}$$ $35 \div 7 =$ $$\begin{array}{r} 13 \\ -6 \\ \hline \end{array}$$ $$\begin{array}{r} 5 \\ \times 3 \\ \hline \end{array}$$

$$\begin{array}{r} 15 \\ -9 \\ \hline \end{array}$$ $27 \div 3 =$ $$\begin{array}{r} 9 \\ \times 6 \\ \hline \end{array}$$ $$\begin{array}{r} 8 \\ \times 7 \\ \hline \end{array}$$ $$\begin{array}{r} 5 \\ +5 \\ \hline \end{array}$$

$$\begin{array}{r} 8 \\ +8 \\ \hline \end{array}$$ $$\begin{array}{r} 9 \\ -3 \\ \hline \end{array}$$ $$\begin{array}{r} 7 \\ +4 \\ \hline \end{array}$$ $72 \div 9 =$ $$\begin{array}{r} 8 \\ \times 4 \\ \hline \end{array}$$

$40 \div 4 =$ $$\begin{array}{r} 6 \\ +6 \\ \hline \end{array}$$ $$\begin{array}{r} 10 \\ -4 \\ \hline \end{array}$$ $$\begin{array}{r} 6 \\ \times 5 \\ \hline \end{array}$$ $$\begin{array}{r} 8 \\ +2 \\ \hline \end{array}$$

Started: _____ Finished: _____ Total Time: _____ Completed: _____ Correct: _____

Name: _____   Date: _____

$9\overline{)18}$

$\begin{array}{r} 9 \\ +\ 3 \\ \hline \end{array}$

$\begin{array}{r} 6 \\ -\ 6 \\ \hline \end{array}$

$8\overline{)32}$

$\begin{array}{r} 7 \\ +\ 4 \\ \hline \end{array}$

$5\overline{)25}$

$\begin{array}{r} 6 \\ +\ 1 \\ \hline \end{array}$

$\begin{array}{r} 4 \\ \times\ 3 \\ \hline \end{array}$

$\begin{array}{r} 4 \\ -\ 4 \\ \hline \end{array}$

$\begin{array}{r} 9 \\ -\ 5 \\ \hline \end{array}$

$4\overline{)16}$

$\begin{array}{r} 2 \\ \times\ 7 \\ \hline \end{array}$

$\begin{array}{r} 15 \\ -\ 6 \\ \hline \end{array}$

$6\overline{)42}$

$\begin{array}{r} 6 \\ +\ 2 \\ \hline \end{array}$

$\begin{array}{r} 5 \\ +\ 9 \\ \hline \end{array}$

$8\overline{)72}$

$\begin{array}{r} 16 \\ -\ 7 \\ \hline \end{array}$

$\begin{array}{r} 9 \\ \times\ 4 \\ \hline \end{array}$

$5\overline{)30}$

$\begin{array}{r} 5 \\ \times\ 2 \\ \hline \end{array}$

$\begin{array}{r} 4 \\ +\ 8 \\ \hline \end{array}$

$6\overline{)18}$

$\begin{array}{r} 8 \\ \times\ 6 \\ \hline \end{array}$

$\begin{array}{r} 7 \\ -\ 3 \\ \hline \end{array}$

$\begin{array}{r} 6 \\ +\ 4 \\ \hline \end{array}$

$\begin{array}{r} 12 \\ -\ 6 \\ \hline \end{array}$

$8\overline{)48}$

$\begin{array}{r} 4 \\ \times\ 9 \\ \hline \end{array}$

$\begin{array}{r} 14 \\ -\ 7 \\ \hline \end{array}$

$\begin{array}{r} 9 \\ +\ 9 \\ \hline \end{array}$

$\begin{array}{r} 9 \\ -\ 2 \\ \hline \end{array}$

$\begin{array}{r} 8 \\ +\ 3 \\ \hline \end{array}$

$\begin{array}{r} 7 \\ \times\ 6 \\ \hline \end{array}$

$7\overline{)56}$

$\begin{array}{r} 8 \\ +\ 9 \\ \hline \end{array}$

$\begin{array}{r} 10 \\ -\ 7 \\ \hline \end{array}$

$\begin{array}{r} 9 \\ \times\ 5 \\ \hline \end{array}$

$3\overline{)24}$

$\begin{array}{r} 7 \\ -\ 6 \\ \hline \end{array}$

Started: Finished: Total Time: Completed: Correct:

Name: _____ Date: _____

$21 \div 3 =$　　$\begin{array}{r} 6 \\ \times\ 3 \\ \hline \end{array}$　　$\begin{array}{r} 8 \\ +\ 7 \\ \hline \end{array}$　　$10 \div 2 =$　　$\begin{array}{r} 12 \\ -\ 5 \\ \hline \end{array}$

$\begin{array}{r} 8 \\ +\ 4 \\ \hline \end{array}$　　$\begin{array}{r} 6 \\ -\ 3 \\ \hline \end{array}$　　$28 \div 4 =$　　$\begin{array}{r} 7 \\ \times\ 3 \\ \hline \end{array}$　　$16 \div 4 =$

$\begin{array}{r} 7 \\ -\ 4 \\ \hline \end{array}$　　$12 \div 3 =$　　$\begin{array}{r} 5 \\ \times\ 3 \\ \hline \end{array}$　　$\begin{array}{r} 8 \\ +\ 2 \\ \hline \end{array}$　　$\begin{array}{r} 10 \\ -\ 0 \\ \hline \end{array}$

$40 \div 5 =$　　$\begin{array}{r} 6 \\ +\ 9 \\ \hline \end{array}$　　$\begin{array}{r} 5 \\ \times\ 4 \\ \hline \end{array}$　　$36 \div 6 =$　　$\begin{array}{r} 14 \\ -\ 5 \\ \hline \end{array}$

$\begin{array}{r} 9 \\ -\ 6 \\ \hline \end{array}$　　$32 \div 8 =$　　$\begin{array}{r} 6 \\ +\ 8 \\ \hline \end{array}$　　$\begin{array}{r} 5 \\ \times\ 5 \\ \hline \end{array}$　　$\begin{array}{r} 7 \\ \times\ 7 \\ \hline \end{array}$

$\begin{array}{r} 9 \\ \times\ 7 \\ \hline \end{array}$　　$10 \div 5 =$　　$\begin{array}{r} 14 \\ -\ 9 \\ \hline \end{array}$　　$28 \div 7 =$　　$\begin{array}{r} 6 \\ +\ 7 \\ \hline \end{array}$

$\begin{array}{r} 16 \\ -\ 5 \\ \hline \end{array}$　　$18 \div 3 =$　　$\begin{array}{r} 7 \\ \times\ 4 \\ \hline \end{array}$　　$\begin{array}{r} 9 \\ \times\ 3 \\ \hline \end{array}$　　$\begin{array}{r} 9 \\ +\ 6 \\ \hline \end{array}$

$\begin{array}{r} 4 \\ +\ 8 \\ \hline \end{array}$　　$\begin{array}{r} 5 \\ +\ 3 \\ \hline \end{array}$　　$\begin{array}{r} 13 \\ -\ 4 \\ \hline \end{array}$　　$\begin{array}{r} 8 \\ \times\ 3 \\ \hline \end{array}$　　$42 \div 6 =$

Started: _____ Finished: _____ Total Time: _____ Completed: _____ Correct: _____

Name: _____   Date: _____

7 $+2$	$9\overline{)81}$	9 $\times 8$	14 -5	9 $+3$
16 -8	$4\overline{)28}$	8 $\times 5$	5 $+9$	15 -7
$5\overline{)20}$	13 -4	4 $+5$	9 $\times 6$	12 -5
7 $+4$	10 -6	$6\overline{)48}$	9 $\times 2$	6 $+5$
6 $\times 7$	7 $\times 2$	13 -9	$5\overline{)45}$	12 $+0$
$4\overline{)36}$	4 $+4$	8 -6	8 $+9$	5 $\times 7$
10 -4	$4\overline{)12}$	7 $\times 3$	7 $+5$	11 -5
8 $+2$	3 $\times 8$	2 $+5$	$7\overline{)35}$	13 -7
$8\overline{)56}$	10 -8	4 $+9$	7 -5	7 $\times 8$
6 $\times 6$	$7\overline{)49}$	8 $\times 8$	11 -7	9 $+7$

Started: _____   Finished: _____   Total Time: _____   Completed: _____   Correct: _____

Name: _____   Date: _____

$$\begin{array}{r} 7 \\ \times\ 3 \\ \hline \end{array}$$
$$\begin{array}{r} 13 \\ -\ 6 \\ \hline \end{array}$$
$$\begin{array}{r} 4 \\ +\ 7 \\ \hline \end{array}$$
$$\begin{array}{r} 8 \\ +\ 6 \\ \hline \end{array}$$
$$36 \div 9 =$$

$$\begin{array}{r} 5 \\ \times\ 5 \\ \hline \end{array}$$
$$\begin{array}{r} 6 \\ +\ 9 \\ \hline \end{array}$$
$$\begin{array}{r} 6 \\ -\ 3 \\ \hline \end{array}$$
$$30 \div 6 =$$
$$\begin{array}{r} 8 \\ \times\ 8 \\ \hline \end{array}$$

$$45 \div 5 =$$
$$\begin{array}{r} 12 \\ -\ 8 \\ \hline \end{array}$$
$$\begin{array}{r} 8 \\ +\ 8 \\ \hline \end{array}$$
$$24 \div 2 =$$
$$\begin{array}{r} 8 \\ \times\ 2 \\ \hline \end{array}$$

$$\begin{array}{r} 9 \\ -\ 0 \\ \hline \end{array}$$
$$\begin{array}{r} 7 \\ +\ 7 \\ \hline \end{array}$$
$$32 \div 8 =$$
$$\begin{array}{r} 7 \\ -\ 2 \\ \hline \end{array}$$
$$\begin{array}{r} 8 \\ \times\ 4 \\ \hline \end{array}$$

$$40 \div 8 =$$
$$\begin{array}{r} 8 \\ +\ 4 \\ \hline \end{array}$$
$$\begin{array}{r} 14 \\ -\ 6 \\ \hline \end{array}$$
$$\begin{array}{r} 3 \\ \times\ 9 \\ \hline \end{array}$$
$$\begin{array}{r} 13 \\ -\ 7 \\ \hline \end{array}$$

$$\begin{array}{r} 8 \\ -\ 5 \\ \hline \end{array}$$
$$\begin{array}{r} 7 \\ \times\ 4 \\ \hline \end{array}$$
$$\begin{array}{r} 9 \\ +\ 9 \\ \hline \end{array}$$
$$\begin{array}{r} 7 \\ \times\ 7 \\ \hline \end{array}$$
$$21 \div 3 =$$

$$\begin{array}{r} 9 \\ +\ 4 \\ \hline \end{array}$$
$$54 \div 9 =$$
$$\begin{array}{r} 2 \\ \times\ 7 \\ \hline \end{array}$$
$$\begin{array}{r} 8 \\ \times\ 6 \\ \hline \end{array}$$
$$\begin{array}{r} 16 \\ -\ 9 \\ \hline \end{array}$$

$$\begin{array}{r} 12 \\ -\ 4 \\ \hline \end{array}$$
$$21 \div 7 =$$
$$\begin{array}{r} 7 \\ +\ 5 \\ \hline \end{array}$$
$$12 \div 4 =$$
$$\begin{array}{r} 5 \\ \times\ 3 \\ \hline \end{array}$$

$$\begin{array}{r} 4 \\ +\ 4 \\ \hline \end{array}$$
$$\begin{array}{r} 11 \\ -\ 5 \\ \hline \end{array}$$
$$18 \div 6 =$$
$$\begin{array}{r} 6 \\ \times\ 9 \\ \hline \end{array}$$
$$42 \div 6 =$$

$$\begin{array}{r} 7 \\ +\ 9 \\ \hline \end{array}$$
$$49 \div 7 =$$
$$\begin{array}{r} 6 \\ \times\ 3 \\ \hline \end{array}$$
$$\begin{array}{r} 14 \\ -\ 5 \\ \hline \end{array}$$
$$\begin{array}{r} 4 \\ +\ 5 \\ \hline \end{array}$$

Started: _____   Finished: _____   Total Time: _____   Completed: _____   Correct: _____

50

Name: _____   Date: _____

$$\begin{array}{r} 6 \\ \times\,6 \\ \hline \end{array} \qquad \begin{array}{r} 3 \\ +\,4 \\ \hline \end{array} \qquad \begin{array}{r} 11 \\ -\,6 \\ \hline \end{array} \qquad 4\overline{)40} \qquad \begin{array}{r} 3 \\ \times\,9 \\ \hline \end{array}$$

$$\begin{array}{r} 8 \\ -\,7 \\ \hline \end{array} \qquad 3\overline{)24} \qquad \begin{array}{r} 6 \\ \times\,7 \\ \hline \end{array} \qquad \begin{array}{r} 8 \\ -\,3 \\ \hline \end{array} \qquad \begin{array}{r} 10 \\ +\,8 \\ \hline \end{array}$$

$$\begin{array}{r} 4 \\ \times\,3 \\ \hline \end{array} \qquad \begin{array}{r} 6 \\ -\,4 \\ \hline \end{array} \qquad \begin{array}{r} 6 \\ +\,0 \\ \hline \end{array} \qquad \begin{array}{r} 12 \\ \times\,4 \\ \hline \end{array} \qquad 7\overline{)35}$$

$$\begin{array}{r} 5 \\ +\,6 \\ \hline \end{array} \qquad \begin{array}{r} 8 \\ -\,4 \\ \hline \end{array} \qquad 9\overline{)63} \qquad \begin{array}{r} 5 \\ \times\,7 \\ \hline \end{array} \qquad \begin{array}{r} 5 \\ -\,3 \\ \hline \end{array}$$

$$5\overline{)15} \qquad \begin{array}{r} 10 \\ \times\,6 \\ \hline \end{array} \qquad \begin{array}{r} 6 \\ -\,3 \\ \hline \end{array} \qquad \begin{array}{r} 6 \\ +\,3 \\ \hline \end{array} \qquad 6\overline{)12}$$

$$5\overline{)45} \qquad 6\overline{)48} \qquad \begin{array}{r} 7 \\ \times\,5 \\ \hline \end{array} \qquad \begin{array}{r} 16 \\ -\,8 \\ \hline \end{array} \qquad \begin{array}{r} 14 \\ -\,7 \\ \hline \end{array}$$

$$\begin{array}{r} 8 \\ \times\,9 \\ \hline \end{array} \qquad \begin{array}{r} 8 \\ +\,4 \\ \hline \end{array} \qquad \begin{array}{r} 6 \\ -\,6 \\ \hline \end{array} \qquad 7\overline{)42} \qquad \begin{array}{r} 6 \\ \times\,9 \\ \hline \end{array}$$

$$\begin{array}{r} 4 \\ \times\,5 \\ \hline \end{array} \qquad \begin{array}{r} 8 \\ +\,6 \\ \hline \end{array} \qquad 8\overline{)40} \qquad \begin{array}{r} 12 \\ -\,6 \\ \hline \end{array} \qquad \begin{array}{r} 8 \\ +\,7 \\ \hline \end{array}$$

$$\begin{array}{r} 3 \\ +\,9 \\ \hline \end{array} \qquad \begin{array}{r} 9 \\ -\,5 \\ \hline \end{array} \qquad 6\overline{)66} \qquad \begin{array}{r} 4 \\ \times\,8 \\ \hline \end{array} \qquad 5\overline{)35}$$

$$6\overline{)36} \qquad \begin{array}{r} 4 \\ \times\,6 \\ \hline \end{array} \qquad \begin{array}{r} 7 \\ -\,4 \\ \hline \end{array} \qquad \begin{array}{r} 6 \\ +\,4 \\ \hline \end{array} \qquad \begin{array}{r} 15 \\ -\,8 \\ \hline \end{array}$$

Started: _____   Finished: _____   Total Time: _____   Completed: _____   Correct: _____

Name: _____   Date: _____

11 − 4	9 + 5	10 × 3	8 − 5	35 ÷ 7 =	8 + 5
54 ÷ 9 =	6 × 7	8 + 8	7 − 5	10 × 9	4 + 0
9 − 2	4 × 5	4 + 8	14 − 5	32 ÷ 8 =	9 + 9
11 − 7	25 ÷ 5 =	9 × 7	10 − 5	8 + 4	6 × 6
15 ÷ 5 =	8 + 2	6 − 3	12 ÷ 6 =	6 × 4	9 × 8
9 × 6	64 ÷ 8 =	4 × 6	15 − 7	7 + 3	8 − 2
72 ÷ 9 =	7 + 8	7 − 6	63 ÷ 9 =	8 × 8	15 − 9
12 − 8	7 × 7	27 ÷ 9 =	9 × 5	7 − 3	9 + 6
8 − 6	6 + 5	3 × 8	4 + 5	7 + 7	28 ÷ 4 =
8 × 4	63 ÷ 7 =	9 × 9	7 + 4	6 − 4	7 + 9

Started: _____   Finished: _____   Total Time: _____   Completed: _____   Correct: _____

Name: _____   Date: _____

13 $-\ 6$	10 $-\ 2$	6 $+\ 4$	12 $-\ 6$	$8\overline{)48}$	4 $\times\ 9$
$5\overline{)45}$	12 $-\ 7$	9 $+\ 8$	$2\overline{)18}$	8 $\times\ 2$	9 $-\ 4$
6 $-\ 5$	3 $+\ 6$	14 $-\ 9$	7 $+\ 5$	$7\overline{)28}$	8 $\times\ 9$
7 $\times\ 7$	$6\overline{)48}$	3 $\times\ 6$	17 $-\ 8$	3 $+\ 4$	11 $-\ 6$
$4\overline{)16}$	7 $\times\ 5$	7 $+\ 6$	12 $-\ 5$	$8\overline{)16}$	7 $\times\ 2$
15 $-\ 9$	6 $\times\ 7$	$9\overline{)36}$	8 $\times\ 5$	7 $-\ 4$	8 $+\ 6$
16 $-\ 8$	6 $+\ 9$	10 $-\ 4$	$7\overline{)56}$	3 $\times\ 9$	5 $+\ 5$
$3\overline{)27}$	12 $-\ 4$	6 $+\ 8$	$2\overline{)14}$	9 $\times\ 2$	6 $+\ 3$
$3\overline{)36}$	10 $+\ 8$	11 $-\ 5$	6 $\times\ 8$	$7\overline{)35}$	5 $+\ 9$
16 $-\ 9$	9 $\times\ 3$	6 $+\ 2$	$3\overline{)21}$	6 $+\ 6$	$6\overline{)24}$

Started: _____   Finished: _____   Total Time: _____   Completed: _____   Correct: _____

Name: _____ Date: _____

Directions: Write each fraction in simplest form.

$\dfrac{2}{4}$ ☐ $\dfrac{2}{6}$ ☐ $\dfrac{7}{14}$ ☐ $\dfrac{3}{9}$ ☐

$\dfrac{6}{9}$ ☐ $\dfrac{9}{18}$ ☐ $\dfrac{9}{12}$ ☐ $\dfrac{12}{24}$ ☐

$\dfrac{2}{8}$ ☐ $\dfrac{4}{12}$ ☐ $\dfrac{6}{18}$ ☐ $\dfrac{8}{16}$ ☐

$\dfrac{3}{15}$ ☐ $\dfrac{10}{20}$ ☐ $\dfrac{2}{10}$ ☐ $\dfrac{8}{12}$ ☐

$\dfrac{6}{8}$ ☐ $\dfrac{6}{6}$ ☐ $\dfrac{5}{10}$ ☐ $\dfrac{8}{14}$ ☐

Started: Finished: Total Time: Completed: Correct:

Name: _____   Date: _____

Directions: Write each fraction in simplest form.

$\dfrac{3}{12}$ ☐ $\dfrac{2}{14}$ ☐ $\dfrac{6}{8}$ ☐ $\dfrac{8}{10}$ ☐

$\dfrac{5}{15}$ ☐ $\dfrac{6}{12}$ ☐ $\dfrac{4}{8}$ ☐ $\dfrac{4}{16}$ ☐

$\dfrac{12}{36}$ ☐ $\dfrac{12}{18}$ ☐ $\dfrac{4}{10}$ ☐ $\dfrac{5}{30}$ ☐

$\dfrac{4}{6}$ ☐ $\dfrac{2}{10}$ ☐ $\dfrac{7}{14}$ ☐ $\dfrac{5}{20}$ ☐

$\dfrac{2}{12}$ ☐ $\dfrac{11}{33}$ ☐ $\dfrac{12}{24}$ ☐ $\dfrac{4}{40}$ ☐

Started: Finished: Total Time: Completed: Correct:

Name: _____ Date: _____

Directions: Write each fraction in simplest form.

$\frac{2}{4}$ ☐ $\frac{5}{10}$ ☐ $\frac{2}{8}$ ☐ $\frac{4}{12}$ ☐ $\frac{6}{18}$ ☐

$\frac{6}{12}$ ☐ $\frac{4}{8}$ ☐ $\frac{5}{15}$ ☐ $\frac{8}{16}$ ☐ $\frac{7}{21}$ ☐

$\frac{11}{22}$ ☐ $\frac{3}{21}$ ☐ $\frac{10}{14}$ ☐ $\frac{3}{12}$ ☐ $\frac{6}{24}$ ☐

$\frac{3}{6}$ ☐ $\frac{14}{16}$ ☐ $\frac{3}{18}$ ☐ $\frac{2}{10}$ ☐ $\frac{5}{25}$ ☐

$\frac{2}{16}$ ☐ $\frac{3}{9}$ ☐ $\frac{4}{28}$ ☐ $\frac{4}{4}$ ☐ $\frac{9}{18}$ ☐

$\frac{2}{2}$ ☐ $\frac{5}{20}$ ☐ $\frac{6}{36}$ ☐ $\frac{7}{28}$ ☐ $\frac{8}{24}$ ☐

Started: Finished: Total Time: Completed: Correct:

Name: _____   Date: _____

Directions: Write each fraction in simplest form.

$\frac{3}{12}$ ☐ $\frac{4}{8}$ ☐ $\frac{6}{10}$ ☐ $\frac{2}{22}$ ☐ $\frac{15}{20}$ ☐

$\frac{3}{9}$ ☐ $\frac{2}{14}$ ☐ $\frac{2}{6}$ ☐ $\frac{3}{24}$ ☐ $\frac{4}{32}$ ☐

$\frac{6}{12}$ ☐ $\frac{2}{18}$ ☐ $\frac{3}{30}$ ☐ $\frac{4}{16}$ ☐ $\frac{5}{5}$ ☐

$\frac{3}{3}$ ☐ $\frac{8}{24}$ ☐ $\frac{5}{10}$ ☐ $\frac{14}{21}$ ☐ $\frac{10}{10}$ ☐

$\frac{4}{24}$ ☐ $\frac{6}{18}$ ☐ $\frac{5}{15}$ ☐ $\frac{3}{6}$ ☐ $\frac{8}{16}$ ☐

$\frac{2}{8}$ ☐ $\frac{5}{30}$ ☐ $\frac{12}{18}$ ☐ $\frac{4}{44}$ ☐ $\frac{7}{49}$ ☐

Started: _____   Finished: _____   Total Time: _____   Completed: _____   Correct: _____

Directions: Write each fraction in simplest form.

$\frac{6}{8}$ ☐ $\frac{5}{55}$ ☐ $\frac{3}{15}$ ☐ $\frac{3}{6}$ ☐ $\frac{2}{10}$ ☐

$\frac{2}{12}$ ☐ $\frac{2}{20}$ ☐ $\frac{2}{2}$ ☐ $\frac{3}{33}$ ☐ $\frac{4}{12}$ ☐

$\frac{3}{21}$ ☐ $\frac{5}{20}$ ☐ $\frac{4}{44}$ ☐ $\frac{6}{30}$ ☐ $\frac{7}{42}$ ☐

$\frac{4}{36}$ ☐ $\frac{6}{24}$ ☐ $\frac{14}{21}$ ☐ $\frac{5}{25}$ ☐ $\frac{3}{18}$ ☐

$\frac{5}{10}$ ☐ $\frac{7}{56}$ ☐ $\frac{8}{24}$ ☐ $\frac{3}{9}$ ☐ $\frac{7}{7}$ ☐

$\frac{6}{18}$ ☐ $\frac{4}{8}$ ☐ $\frac{12}{18}$ ☐ $\frac{4}{48}$ ☐ $\frac{12}{24}$ ☐

$\frac{8}{14}$ ☐ $\frac{10}{20}$ ☐ $\frac{4}{14}$ ☐ $\frac{3}{24}$ ☐ $\frac{9}{18}$ ☐

$\frac{10}{12}$ ☐ $\frac{7}{28}$ ☐ $\frac{16}{20}$ ☐ $\frac{3}{12}$ ☐ $\frac{25}{35}$ ☐

Started: Finished: Total Time: Completed: Correct:

Name: _____ Date: _____

Directions: Write each fraction in simplest form.

$\frac{3}{9}$ ☐ $\frac{2}{24}$ ☐ $\frac{8}{32}$ ☐ $\frac{4}{40}$ ☐ $\frac{20}{28}$ ☐

$\frac{2}{4}$ ☐ $\frac{3}{18}$ ☐ $\frac{4}{28}$ ☐ $\frac{5}{55}$ ☐ $\frac{6}{10}$ ☐

$\frac{2}{12}$ ☐ $\frac{12}{36}$ ☐ $\frac{5}{15}$ ☐ $\frac{8}{8}$ ☐ $\frac{18}{36}$ ☐

$\frac{8}{12}$ ☐ $\frac{3}{24}$ ☐ $\frac{4}{20}$ ☐ $\frac{9}{27}$ ☐ $\frac{6}{18}$ ☐

$\frac{9}{9}$ ☐ $\frac{6}{14}$ ☐ $\frac{4}{32}$ ☐ $\frac{9}{36}$ ☐ $\frac{18}{20}$ ☐

$\frac{4}{48}$ ☐ $\frac{20}{20}$ ☐ $\frac{3}{27}$ ☐ $\frac{5}{60}$ ☐ $\frac{4}{30}$ ☐

$\frac{6}{36}$ ☐ $\frac{8}{14}$ ☐ $\frac{2}{22}$ ☐ $\frac{4}{36}$ ☐ $\frac{27}{30}$ ☐

$\frac{8}{10}$ ☐ $\frac{9}{21}$ ☐ $\frac{6}{8}$ ☐ $\frac{8}{18}$ ☐ $\frac{8}{20}$ ☐

Started: _____ Finished: _____ Total Time: _____ Completed: _____ Correct: _____

Name: _____   Date: _____

Directions: Write each fraction in simplest form. Answers will be whole numbers, reduced fractions, or mixed numbers.

$\dfrac{9}{3}$ ▢ $\dfrac{25}{15}$ ▢ $\dfrac{12}{3}$ ▢ $\dfrac{9}{6}$ ▢

$\dfrac{10}{8}$ ▢ $\dfrac{8}{5}$ ▢ $\dfrac{16}{12}$ ▢ $\dfrac{5}{4}$ ▢

$\dfrac{6}{2}$ ▢ $\dfrac{16}{14}$ ▢ $\dfrac{13}{6}$ ▢ $\dfrac{7}{5}$ ▢

$\dfrac{24}{9}$ ▢ $\dfrac{21}{9}$ ▢ $\dfrac{18}{6}$ ▢ $\dfrac{17}{5}$ ▢

$\dfrac{3}{2}$ ▢ $\dfrac{15}{4}$ ▢ $\dfrac{10}{2}$ ▢ $\dfrac{21}{3}$ ▢

Started: Finished: Total Time: Completed: Correct:

Name: _____ Date: _____

Directions: Write each fraction in simplest form. Answers will be whole numbers, reduced fractions, or mixed numbers.

$\frac{30}{6}$ ☐ $\frac{10}{6}$ ☐ $\frac{16}{4}$ ☐ $\frac{32}{16}$ ☐

$\frac{18}{14}$ ☐ $\frac{7}{2}$ ☐ $\frac{50}{15}$ ☐ $\frac{15}{5}$ ☐

$\frac{20}{4}$ ☐ $\frac{7}{4}$ ☐ $\frac{12}{6}$ ☐ $\frac{20}{8}$ ☐

$\frac{48}{6}$ ☐ $\frac{32}{8}$ ☐ $\frac{22}{5}$ ☐ $\frac{15}{7}$ ☐

$\frac{15}{6}$ ☐ $\frac{8}{6}$ ☐ $\frac{18}{3}$ ☐ $\frac{9}{6}$ ☐

Started: _____   Finished: _____   Total Time: _____   Completed: _____   Correct: _____

Name: _____ Date: _____

Directions: Write each fraction in simplest form. Answers will be whole numbers, reduced fractions, or mixed numbers.

$\dfrac{19}{12}$ ☐ $\dfrac{3}{2}$ ☐ $\dfrac{12}{8}$ ☐ $\dfrac{25}{5}$ ☐ $\dfrac{10}{7}$ ☐

$\dfrac{7}{4}$ ☐ $\dfrac{18}{12}$ ☐ $\dfrac{10}{3}$ ☐ $\dfrac{49}{7}$ ☐ $\dfrac{33}{6}$ ☐

$\dfrac{9}{8}$ ☐ $\dfrac{15}{7}$ ☐ $\dfrac{12}{4}$ ☐ $\dfrac{17}{6}$ ☐ $\dfrac{12}{10}$ ☐

$\dfrac{13}{12}$ ☐ $\dfrac{30}{15}$ ☐ $\dfrac{8}{3}$ ☐ $\dfrac{18}{16}$ ☐ $\dfrac{15}{9}$ ☐

$\dfrac{12}{9}$ ☐ $\dfrac{6}{4}$ ☐ $\dfrac{18}{9}$ ☐ $\dfrac{5}{3}$ ☐ $\dfrac{36}{9}$ ☐

$\dfrac{8}{6}$ ☐ $\dfrac{9}{6}$ ☐ $\dfrac{16}{14}$ ☐ $\dfrac{35}{20}$ ☐ $\dfrac{14}{7}$ ☐

Started: _____   Finished: _____   Total Time: _____   Completed: _____   Correct: _____

Name: _____ Date: _____

Directions: Write each fraction in simplest form. Answers will be whole numbers, reduced fractions, or mixed numbers.

$\frac{9}{3}$ ☐ $\frac{10}{8}$ ☐ $\frac{18}{12}$ ☐ $\frac{7}{3}$ ☐ $\frac{15}{3}$ ☐

$\frac{14}{12}$ ☐ $\frac{15}{5}$ ☐ $\frac{28}{7}$ ☐ $\frac{12}{8}$ ☐ $\frac{50}{8}$ ☐

$\frac{18}{16}$ ☐ $\frac{20}{10}$ ☐ $\frac{18}{6}$ ☐ $\frac{23}{7}$ ☐ $\frac{9}{5}$ ☐

$\frac{19}{9}$ ☐ $\frac{20}{5}$ ☐ $\frac{19}{6}$ ☐ $\frac{21}{7}$ ☐ $\frac{24}{6}$ ☐

$\frac{14}{3}$ ☐ $\frac{17}{5}$ ☐ $\frac{8}{4}$ ☐ $\frac{40}{10}$ ☐ $\frac{64}{8}$ ☐

$\frac{10}{3}$ ☐ $\frac{27}{12}$ ☐ $\frac{16}{5}$ ☐ $\frac{35}{7}$ ☐ $\frac{32}{5}$ ☐

Started: _____ Finished: _____ Total Time: _____ Completed: _____ Correct: _____

Name: _____   Date: _____

Directions: Write each fraction in simplest form. Answers will be whole numbers, reduced fractions, or mixed numbers.

$\frac{3}{2}$ ☐ $\frac{48}{12}$ ☐ $\frac{24}{9}$ ☐ $\frac{33}{10}$ ☐ $\frac{20}{5}$ ☐

$\frac{10}{4}$ ☐ $\frac{8}{3}$ ☐ $\frac{32}{8}$ ☐ $\frac{9}{5}$ ☐ $\frac{11}{10}$ ☐

$\frac{14}{7}$ ☐ $\frac{20}{4}$ ☐ $\frac{12}{5}$ ☐ $\frac{24}{4}$ ☐ $\frac{18}{14}$ ☐

$\frac{50}{10}$ ☐ $\frac{15}{5}$ ☐ $\frac{30}{6}$ ☐ $\frac{10}{7}$ ☐ $\frac{7}{6}$ ☐

$\frac{16}{4}$ ☐ $\frac{21}{14}$ ☐ $\frac{45}{15}$ ☐ $\frac{24}{3}$ ☐ $\frac{22}{11}$ ☐

$\frac{18}{10}$ ☐ $\frac{35}{7}$ ☐ $\frac{49}{7}$ ☐ $\frac{8}{5}$ ☐ $\frac{60}{30}$ ☐

$\frac{36}{6}$ ☐ $\frac{7}{2}$ ☐ $\frac{16}{8}$ ☐ $\frac{36}{9}$ ☐ $\frac{12}{8}$ ☐

$\frac{5}{2}$ ☐ $\frac{24}{12}$ ☐ $\frac{15}{9}$ ☐ $\frac{32}{6}$ ☐ $\frac{28}{14}$ ☐

Started: _____   Finished: _____   Total Time: _____   Completed: _____   Correct: _____

Name: _____   Date: _____

Directions: Write each fraction in simplest form. Answers will be whole numbers, reduced fractions, or mixed numbers.

$\frac{50}{25}$ ☐ $\frac{10}{7}$ ☐ $\frac{24}{16}$ ☐ $\frac{7}{4}$ ☐ $\frac{18}{12}$ ☐

$\frac{14}{7}$ ☐ $\frac{8}{3}$ ☐ $\frac{27}{9}$ ☐ $\frac{18}{3}$ ☐ $\frac{12}{4}$ ☐

$\frac{21}{3}$ ☐ $\frac{32}{8}$ ☐ $\frac{20}{12}$ ☐ $\frac{33}{24}$ ☐ $\frac{10}{8}$ ☐

$\frac{36}{9}$ ☐ $\frac{24}{8}$ ☐ $\frac{9}{4}$ ☐ $\frac{15}{6}$ ☐ $\frac{8}{4}$ ☐

$\frac{16}{10}$ ☐ $\frac{21}{18}$ ☐ $\frac{16}{14}$ ☐ $\frac{7}{5}$ ☐ $\frac{40}{15}$ ☐

$\frac{6}{4}$ ☐ $\frac{16}{4}$ ☐ $\frac{15}{10}$ ☐ $\frac{9}{3}$ ☐ $\frac{20}{15}$ ☐

$\frac{16}{8}$ ☐ $\frac{7}{6}$ ☐ $\frac{5}{4}$ ☐ $\frac{15}{3}$ ☐ $\frac{4}{2}$ ☐

$\frac{28}{14}$ ☐ $\frac{8}{2}$ ☐ $\frac{16}{10}$ ☐ $\frac{22}{10}$ ☐ $\frac{48}{24}$ ☐

Started: _____   Finished: _____   Total Time: _____   Completed: _____   Correct: _____

Name: _____ Date: _____

Directions: Write each fraction in simplest form. Answers will be whole numbers, reduced fractions, or mixed numbers.

$\dfrac{4}{10}$ ☐ $\dfrac{5}{3}$ ☐ $\dfrac{11}{7}$ ☐ $\dfrac{10}{22}$ ☐

$\dfrac{5}{30}$ ☐ $\dfrac{7}{2}$ ☐ $\dfrac{8}{16}$ ☐ $\dfrac{12}{5}$ ☐

$\dfrac{42}{8}$ ☐ $\dfrac{44}{11}$ ☐ $\dfrac{10}{12}$ ☐ $\dfrac{9}{18}$ ☐

$\dfrac{8}{20}$ ☐ $\dfrac{25}{5}$ ☐ $\dfrac{12}{36}$ ☐ $\dfrac{12}{48}$ ☐

$\dfrac{72}{9}$ ☐ $\dfrac{15}{35}$ ☐ $\dfrac{33}{4}$ ☐ $\dfrac{9}{2}$ ☐

Started: _____   Finished: _____   Total Time: _____   Completed: _____   Correct: _____

Name: _____   Date: _____

Directions: Write each fraction in simplest form. Answers will be whole numbers, reduced fractions, or mixed numbers.

$\dfrac{11}{4}$ ☐ $\dfrac{3}{9}$ ☐ $\dfrac{10}{8}$ ☐ $\dfrac{14}{5}$ ☐

$\dfrac{6}{15}$ ☐ $\dfrac{12}{2}$ ☐ $\dfrac{18}{10}$ ☐ $\dfrac{4}{20}$ ☐

$\dfrac{16}{8}$ ☐ $\dfrac{6}{18}$ ☐ $\dfrac{32}{8}$ ☐ $\dfrac{22}{10}$ ☐

$\dfrac{2}{12}$ ☐ $\dfrac{8}{4}$ ☐ $\dfrac{18}{30}$ ☐ $\dfrac{21}{7}$ ☐

$\dfrac{16}{5}$ ☐ $\dfrac{9}{27}$ ☐ $\dfrac{48}{8}$ ☐ $\dfrac{10}{30}$ ☐

Started: _____   Finished: _____   Total Time: _____   Completed: _____   Correct: _____

Name: _____ Date: _____

Directions: Write each fraction in simplest form. Answers will be whole numbers, reduced fractions, or mixed numbers.

$\frac{49}{7}$ ☐ $\frac{6}{8}$ ☐ $\frac{11}{9}$ ☐ $\frac{10}{18}$ ☐ $\frac{12}{6}$ ☐

$\frac{7}{2}$ ☐ $\frac{10}{20}$ ☐ $\frac{12}{8}$ ☐ $\frac{4}{24}$ ☐ $\frac{11}{33}$ ☐

$\frac{3}{9}$ ☐ $\frac{8}{6}$ ☐ $\frac{30}{10}$ ☐ $\frac{7}{21}$ ☐ $\frac{4}{36}$ ☐

$\frac{9}{24}$ ☐ $\frac{10}{10}$ ☐ $\frac{18}{9}$ ☐ $\frac{15}{7}$ ☐ $\frac{24}{3}$ ☐

$\frac{6}{1}$ ☐ $\frac{20}{4}$ ☐ $\frac{9}{2}$ ☐ $\frac{32}{16}$ ☐ $\frac{14}{18}$ ☐

$\frac{72}{8}$ ☐ $\frac{16}{32}$ ☐ $\frac{13}{10}$ ☐ $\frac{18}{20}$ ☐ $\frac{9}{3}$ ☐

Started: Finished: Total Time: Completed: Correct:

Name: _____   Date: _____

Directions: Write each fraction in simplest form. Answers will be whole numbers, reduced fractions, or mixed numbers.

$\frac{35}{5}$ ☐ $\frac{6}{10}$ ☐ $\frac{10}{15}$ ☐ $\frac{24}{9}$ ☐ $\frac{7}{7}$ ☐

$\frac{6}{24}$ ☐ $\frac{9}{2}$ ☐ $\frac{5}{10}$ ☐ $\frac{9}{27}$ ☐ $\frac{28}{4}$ ☐

$\frac{18}{9}$ ☐ $\frac{4}{20}$ ☐ $\frac{12}{6}$ ☐ $\frac{18}{15}$ ☐ $\frac{40}{10}$ ☐

$\frac{3}{1}$ ☐ $\frac{16}{24}$ ☐ $\frac{21}{2}$ ☐ $\frac{32}{6}$ ☐ $\frac{5}{15}$ ☐

$\frac{21}{7}$ ☐ $\frac{18}{3}$ ☐ $\frac{55}{5}$ ☐ $\frac{8}{6}$ ☐ $\frac{14}{24}$ ☐

$\frac{27}{18}$ ☐ $\frac{9}{36}$ ☐ $\frac{33}{10}$ ☐ $\frac{9}{18}$ ☐ $\frac{3}{27}$ ☐

Started: Finished: Total Time: Completed: Correct:

Name: _____ Date: _____

Directions: Write each fraction in simplest form. Answers will be whole numbers, reduced fractions, or mixed numbers.

$\dfrac{4}{4}$ ☐ $\dfrac{16}{4}$ ☐ $\dfrac{9}{3}$ ☐ $\dfrac{24}{8}$ ☐ $\dfrac{9}{1}$ ☐

$\dfrac{6}{12}$ ☐ $\dfrac{50}{15}$ ☐ $\dfrac{18}{14}$ ☐ $\dfrac{3}{2}$ ☐ $\dfrac{14}{7}$ ☐

$\dfrac{12}{3}$ ☐ $\dfrac{6}{8}$ ☐ $\dfrac{2}{16}$ ☐ $\dfrac{30}{6}$ ☐ $\dfrac{2}{20}$ ☐

$\dfrac{21}{15}$ ☐ $\dfrac{36}{4}$ ☐ $\dfrac{7}{21}$ ☐ $\dfrac{28}{7}$ ☐ $\dfrac{15}{12}$ ☐

$\dfrac{9}{27}$ ☐ $\dfrac{4}{8}$ ☐ $\dfrac{18}{27}$ ☐ $\dfrac{9}{36}$ ☐ $\dfrac{24}{6}$ ☐

$\dfrac{12}{6}$ ☐ $\dfrac{20}{8}$ ☐ $\dfrac{16}{8}$ ☐ $\dfrac{7}{35}$ ☐ $\dfrac{18}{9}$ ☐

$\dfrac{10}{12}$ ☐ $\dfrac{4}{6}$ ☐ $\dfrac{18}{5}$ ☐ $\dfrac{12}{7}$ ☐ $\dfrac{16}{32}$ ☐

$\dfrac{40}{20}$ ☐ $\dfrac{8}{18}$ ☐ $\dfrac{10}{90}$ ☐ $\dfrac{5}{3}$ ☐ $\dfrac{9}{9}$ ☐

Started: _____ Finished: _____ Total Time: _____ Completed: _____ Correct: _____

Name: _____ Date: _____

Directions: Write each fraction in simplest form. Answers will be whole numbers, reduced fractions, or mixed numbers.

$\frac{11}{3}$ ☐ $\frac{8}{6}$ ☐ $\frac{15}{4}$ ☐ $\frac{24}{12}$ ☐ $\frac{3}{18}$ ☐

$\frac{4}{12}$ ☐ $\frac{6}{6}$ ☐ $\frac{18}{9}$ ☐ $\frac{16}{18}$ ☐ $\frac{8}{3}$ ☐

$\frac{22}{10}$ ☐ $\frac{11}{44}$ ☐ $\frac{15}{21}$ ☐ $\frac{7}{3}$ ☐ $\frac{6}{24}$ ☐

$\frac{28}{16}$ ☐ $\frac{5}{25}$ ☐ $\frac{8}{4}$ ☐ $\frac{2}{12}$ ☐ $\frac{64}{8}$ ☐

$\frac{9}{45}$ ☐ $\frac{24}{4}$ ☐ $\frac{18}{15}$ ☐ $\frac{25}{30}$ ☐ $\frac{7}{14}$ ☐

$\frac{5}{4}$ ☐ $\frac{49}{56}$ ☐ $\frac{3}{30}$ ☐ $\frac{16}{4}$ ☐ $\frac{24}{6}$ ☐

$\frac{10}{18}$ ☐ $\frac{36}{12}$ ☐ $\frac{7}{6}$ ☐ $\frac{15}{8}$ ☐ $\frac{10}{10}$ ☐

$\frac{30}{5}$ ☐ $\frac{9}{6}$ ☐ $\frac{42}{48}$ ☐ $\frac{15}{14}$ ☐ $\frac{10}{8}$ ☐

Started: _____ Finished: _____ Total Time: _____ Completed: _____ Correct: _____

Name: _____   Date: _____

Directions: Write each value as a fraction in simplest form. Answers will be reduced fractions, whole numbers, or mixed numbers.

0.25 ☐   10% ☐   0.5 ☐   70% ☐

5% ☐   0.9 ☐   20% ☐   0.09 ☐

0.2 ☐   150% ☐   0.15 ☐   75% ☐

15% ☐   0.6 ☐   40% ☐   2.75 ☐

0.7 ☐   30% ☐   0.55 ☐   200% ☐

Started: _____   Finished: _____   Total Time: _____   Completed: _____   Correct: _____

Name: _____   Date: _____

Directions: Write each value as a fraction in simplest form. Answers will be reduced fractions, whole numbers, or mixed numbers.

100% ☐   0.01 ☐   16% ☐   0.33 ☐

0.07 ☐   80% ☐   2.25 ☐   300% ☐

20% ☐   0.5 ☐   90% ☐   2.5 ☐

1.75 ☐   40% ☐   0.005 ☐   150% ☐

75% ☐   0.9 ☐   10% ☐   1.5 ☐

Started: _____   Finished: _____   Total Time: _____   Completed: _____   Correct: _____

Name: _____   Date: _____

Directions: Write each value as a fraction in simplest form. Answers will be reduced fractions, whole numbers, or mixed numbers.

1.25 ☐   23% ☐   0.8 ☐   25% ☐   0.6 ☐

200% ☐   0.3 ☐   15% ☐   2.5 ☐   30% ☐

0.7 ☐   5% ☐   0.75 ☐   20% ☐   1.5 ☐

100% ☐   0.25 ☐   10% ☐   2.25 ☐   40% ☐

0.45 ☐   60% ☐   0.006 ☐   12% ☐   0.5 ☐

55% ☐   0.04 ☐   90% ☐   0.55 ☐   50% ☐

Started: _____   Finished: _____   Total Time: _____   Completed: _____   Correct: _____

Name: _____ Date: _____

Directions: Write each value as a fraction in simplest form. Answers will be reduced fractions, whole numbers, or mixed numbers.

25% ☐   0.09 ☐   50% ☐   0.15 ☐   85% ☐

2.25 ☐   400% ☐   1.25 ☐   11% ☐   0.8 ☐

17% ☐   0.08 ☐   45% ☐   0.02 ☐   19% ☐

1.5 ☐   10% ☐   0.6 ☐   67% ☐   0.03 ☐

35% ☐   0.5 ☐   65% ☐   0.95 ☐   18% ☐

0.85 ☐   21% ☐   0.75 ☐   200% ☐   70% ☐

Started: Finished: Total Time: Completed: Correct:

Name: _____ Date: _____

Directions: Write each value as a fraction in simplest form. Answers will be reduced fractions, whole numbers, or mixed numbers.

40% ☐   2.5 ☐   50% ☐   0.25 ☐   60% ☐

1.25 ☐   26% ☐   0.85 ☐   55% ☐   0.4 ☐

800% ☐   0.6 ☐   15% ☐   6.5 ☐   20% ☐

0.3 ☐   5% ☐   0.75 ☐   75% ☐   3.5 ☐

300% ☐   0.35 ☐   30% ☐   2.25 ☐   10% ☐

0.15 ☐   70% ☐   0.005 ☐   19% ☐   0.9 ☐

65% ☐   0.03 ☐   80% ☐   0.55 ☐   25% ☐

2.75 ☐   35% ☐   0.1 ☐   90% ☐   0.01 ☐

Started: _____ Finished: _____ Total Time: _____ Completed: _____ Correct: _____

Name: _____   Date: _____

Directions: Write each value as a fraction in simplest form. Answers will be reduced fractions, whole numbers, or mixed numbers.

0.004 [ ]   30% [ ]   1.15 [ ]   150% [ ]   2.5 [ ]

5% [ ]   0.09 [ ]   50% [ ]   0.15 [ ]   85% [ ]

2.25 [ ]   21% [ ]   0.29 [ ]   200% [ ]   47% [ ]

600% [ ]   1.25 [ ]   11% [ ]   0.05 [ ]   18% [ ]

17% [ ]   0.08 [ ]   45% [ ]   0.04 [ ]   19% [ ]

1.5 [ ]   10% [ ]   0.6 [ ]   65% [ ]   0.07 [ ]

35% [ ]   0.5 [ ]   83% [ ]   0.75 [ ]   25% [ ]

0.85 [ ]   33% [ ]   0.12 [ ]   0.3 [ ]   0.9 [ ]

Started: _____   Finished: _____   Total Time: _____   Completed: _____   Correct: _____

Name: _____   Date: _____

Directions: Write each value as a decimal.

$\frac{1}{2}$ ☐   23% ☐ $\frac{8}{10}$ ☐   25% ☐

19% ☐ $\frac{8}{100}$ ☐   50% ☐ $\frac{5}{10}$ ☐

$\frac{25}{100}$ ☐   75% ☐ $\frac{2}{5}$ ☐   30% ☐

70% ☐ $1\frac{4}{5}$ ☐   85% ☐   60% ☐

$\frac{9}{12}$ ☐   45% ☐ $\frac{1}{4}$ ☐   2% ☐

Started: Finished: Total Time: Completed: Correct:

Name: _____   Date: _____

Directions: Write each value as a decimal.

30% ☐ $\frac{3}{100}$ ☐   10% ☐ $\frac{3}{5}$ ☐

$\frac{1}{2}$ ☐   200% ☐ $\frac{9}{10}$ ☐   15% ☐

$1\frac{3}{4}$ ☐   150% ☐ $\frac{1}{20}$ ☐   40% ☐

55% ☐ $2\frac{3}{4}$ ☐   26% ☐ $\frac{5}{100}$ ☐

$\frac{11}{20}$ ☐   20% ☐ $\frac{18}{100}$ ☐   80% ☐

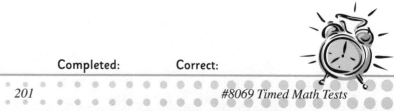

Started: _____   Finished: _____   Total Time: _____   Completed: _____   Correct: _____

Name: _____   **Date:** _____

Directions: Write each value as a decimal.

1% ☐ $\frac{2}{25}$ ☐   45% ☐ $\frac{1}{50}$ ☐   10% ☐

$\frac{17}{20}$ ☐   30% ☐ $\frac{9}{12}$ ☐   150% ☐ $\frac{13}{20}$ ☐

800% ☐ $\frac{1}{5}$ ☐   15% ☐ $6\frac{1}{2}$ ☐   20% ☐

$1\frac{1}{2}$ ☐   70% ☐ $\frac{6}{10}$ ☐   65% ☐ $\frac{3}{4}$ ☐

35% ☐ $\frac{1}{2}$ ☐   83% ☐ $\frac{9}{15}$ ☐   25% ☐

$\frac{7}{10}$ ☐   55% ☐ $\frac{19}{20}$ ☐   40% ☐ $\frac{15}{10}$ ☐

Started: _____ **Finished:** _____ **Total Time:** _____ **Completed:** _____ **Correct:** _____

Name: _____   **Date:** _____

Directions: Write each value as a decimal.

100% ☐ $\frac{1}{4}$ ☐   10% ☐ $\frac{1}{1,000}$ ☐   40% ☐

$\frac{63}{100}$ ☐   20% ☐ $\frac{6}{100}$ ☐   65% ☐ $\frac{6}{8}$ ☐

$\frac{7}{20}$ ☐   33% ☐ $\frac{3}{25}$ ☐ $\frac{33}{100}$ ☐   9% ☐

14% ☐ $\frac{7}{100}$ ☐   50% ☐ $\frac{15}{100}$ ☐   85% ☐

$\frac{6}{10}$ ☐   5% ☐ $\frac{3}{4}$ ☐   70% ☐ $5\frac{1}{2}$ ☐

17% ☐ $\frac{2}{25}$ ☐   45% ☐ $\frac{1}{25}$ ☐   19% ☐

Started: **Finished:**   **Total Time:**   **Completed:**   **Correct:**

Name: _____   Date: _____

Directions: Write each value as a decimal.

$\frac{5}{20}$ ☐   25% ☐ $\frac{1}{4}$ ☐   55% ☐ $1\frac{3}{6}$ ☐

99% ☐ $\frac{5}{10}$ ☐   66% ☐ $\frac{8}{16}$ ☐   33% ☐

$\frac{2}{20}$ ☐   60% ☐ $\frac{3}{1,000}$ ☐   17% ☐ $\frac{1}{2}$ ☐

65% ☐ $\frac{19}{20}$ ☐   18% ☐ $\frac{1}{5}$ ☐   35% ☐

$2\frac{3}{4}$ ☐   85% ☐ $\frac{1}{10}$ ☐   90% ☐ $\frac{1}{100}$ ☐

700% ☐ $\frac{9}{20}$ ☐   30% ☐ $\frac{4}{10}$ ☐   10% ☐

$2\frac{1}{4}$ ☐   21% ☐ $\frac{3}{4}$ ☐   200% ☐   43% ☐

600% ☐ $\frac{4}{100}$ ☐   11% ☐ $\frac{2}{25}$ ☐   70% ☐

Started: _____   Finished: _____   Total Time: _____   Completed: _____   Correct: _____

Name: _____ Date: _____

Directions: Write each value as a decimal.

$\frac{1}{20}$ ☐   18% ☐ $\frac{1}{5}$ ☐   22% ☐ $\frac{1}{4}$ ☐

90% ☐ $\frac{11}{20}$ ☐   50% ☐   55% ☐ $\frac{1}{25}$ ☐

$\frac{17}{20}$ ☐   43% ☐ $\frac{3}{4}$ ☐   100% ☐ $\frac{6}{10}$ ☐

45% ☐ $\frac{19}{100}$ ☐   44% ☐ $\frac{2}{10}$ ☐   99% ☐

$\frac{12}{8}$ ☐   70% ☐ $\frac{5}{100}$ ☐   19% ☐ $\frac{9}{100}$ ☐

65% ☐ $\frac{6}{24}$ ☐   80% ☐ $\frac{55}{100}$ ☐   20% ☐

$\frac{68}{100}$ ☐   12% ☐ $\frac{333}{1,000}$ ☐   66% ☐ $\frac{7}{10}$ ☐

75% ☐ $2\frac{3}{4}$ ☐   10% ☐ $\frac{13}{20}$ ☐   4% ☐

Started: _____ Finished: _____ Total Time: _____ Completed: _____ Correct: _____

Name: _____   Date: _____

Directions: Write each value as a percent.

$\dfrac{4}{10}$ ☐ %   0.5 ☐ % $\dfrac{1}{20}$ ☐ %   0.06 ☐ %

0.2 ☐ % $\dfrac{3}{4}$ ☐ %   0.36 ☐ % $\dfrac{2}{10}$ ☐ %

$\dfrac{7}{14}$ ☐ %   0.9 ☐ % $\dfrac{5}{25}$ ☐ %   0.45 ☐ %

0.11 ☐ % $\dfrac{3}{100}$ ☐ %   1.75 ☐ % $\dfrac{1}{4}$ ☐ %

$\dfrac{2}{5}$ ☐ %   0.55 ☐ % $\dfrac{6}{100}$ ☐ %   0.03 ☐ %

Name: _____   **Date:** _____

Directions: Write each value as a percent.

0.02 ☐ % $\dfrac{3}{5}$ ☐ %   0.13 ☐ % $1\frac{1}{4}$ ☐ %

$\dfrac{1}{25}$ ☐ %   0.8 ☐ % $\dfrac{3}{10}$ ☐ %   2.5 ☐ %

0.9 ☐ % $2\frac{3}{4}$ ☐ %   2.25 ☐ % $\dfrac{2}{100}$ ☐ %

$\dfrac{3}{4}$ ☐ %   0.18 ☐ % $\dfrac{4}{5}$ ☐ %   4.5 ☐ %

0.01 ☐ % $\dfrac{9}{20}$ ☐ %   0.004 ☐ % $\dfrac{4}{10}$ ☐ %

Started: Finished: Total Time: Completed: Correct:

Name: _____ Date: _____

Directions: Write each value as a percent.

$1\frac{1}{2}$ ☐ %   0.7 ☐ % $\frac{13}{100}$ ☐ %   3.5 ☐ % $\frac{4}{5}$ ☐ %

1.75 ☐ % $\frac{73}{100}$ ☐ %   0.18 ☐ % $\frac{9}{10}$ ☐ %   0.1 ☐ %

$\frac{1}{10}$ ☐ %   0.6 ☐ % $\frac{33}{100}$ ☐ %   0.01 ☐ % $\frac{3}{10}$ ☐ %

0.25 ☐ % $\frac{8}{20}$ ☐ %   0.22 ☐ % $\frac{3}{20}$ ☐ %   2.75 ☐ %

$\frac{5}{20}$ ☐ %   1.5 ☐ % $\frac{1}{25}$ ☐ %   2.25 ☐ % $\frac{19}{100}$ ☐ %

0.33 ☐ % $\frac{7}{10}$ ☐ %   0.5 ☐ % $1\frac{3}{4}$ ☐ %   0.38 ☐ %

Started: _____ Finished: _____ Total Time: _____ Completed: _____ Correct: _____

Name: _____ **Date:** _____

Directions: Write each value as a percent.

$\dfrac{1}{2}$ ☐ %   0.5 ☐ % $\dfrac{3}{10}$ ☐ %   1.33 ☐ % $\dfrac{2}{5}$ ☐ %

0.9 ☐ % $\dfrac{1}{4}$ ☐ %   0.77 ☐ % $\dfrac{1}{25}$ ☐ %   0.18 ☐ %

$\dfrac{3}{4}$ ☐ %   0.16 ☐ % $\dfrac{1}{20}$ ☐ %   0.95 ☐ % $\dfrac{4}{20}$ ☐ %

0.04 ☐ % $\dfrac{1}{10}$ ☐ %   2.25 ☐ % $\dfrac{17}{20}$ ☐ %   1.75 ☐ %

$\dfrac{1}{5}$ ☐ %   0.06 ☐ % $\dfrac{3}{4}$ ☐ %   0.25 ☐ % $\dfrac{15}{20}$ ☐ %

0.05 ☐ % $\dfrac{9}{10}$ ☐ %   0.15 ☐ % $\dfrac{28}{100}$ ☐ %   0.2 ☐ %

Started: _____ **Finished:** _____ **Total Time:** _____ **Completed:** _____ **Correct:** _____

Name: _____   Date: _____

Directions: Write each value as a percent.

$1\frac{4}{5}$ [ ] %   0.13 [ ] % $\frac{2}{5}$ [ ] %   0.17 [ ] % $1\frac{1}{2}$ [ ] %

0.009 [ ] % $\frac{15}{25}$ [ ] %   0.4 [ ] % $\frac{13}{20}$ [ ] %   0.12 [ ] %

$2\frac{3}{5}$ [ ] %   2.5 [ ] % $1\frac{3}{5}$ [ ] %   0.33 [ ] % $\frac{100}{100}$ [ ] %

0.003 [ ] %   1 [ ] %   0.21 [ ] % $\frac{12}{24}$ [ ] % $\frac{3}{5}$ [ ] %

$\frac{7}{10}$ [ ] %   0.9 [ ] % $2\frac{3}{4}$ [ ] %   2.25 [ ] % $\frac{2}{100}$ [ ] %

0.45 [ ] % $\frac{5}{25}$ [ ] %   3.7 [ ] % $\frac{11}{20}$ [ ] %   0.55 [ ] %

$\frac{6}{8}$ [ ] %   0.6 [ ] % $\frac{3}{100}$ [ ] %   0.04 [ ] % $\frac{3}{10}$ [ ] %

0.95 [ ] % $\frac{50}{100}$ [ ] %   0.89 [ ] % $\frac{6}{30}$ [ ] %   0.23 [ ] %

Started: _____   Finished: _____   Total Time: _____   Completed: _____   Correct: _____

Name: _____   Date: _____

Directions: Write each value as a percent.

0.1 [ ] % $\frac{9}{10}$ [ ] %   1.33 [ ] % $\frac{7}{20}$ [ ] %   2.25 [ ] %

$\frac{7}{100}$ [ ] %   0.09 [ ] % $\frac{2}{5}$ [ ] %   0.15 [ ] % $\frac{3}{4}$ [ ] %

0.29 [ ] % $2\frac{3}{5}$ [ ] %   0.05 [ ] % $\frac{13}{100}$ [ ] %   0.47 [ ] %

$\frac{1}{25}$ [ ] %   0.25 [ ] % $\frac{10}{100}$ [ ] %   0.02 [ ] % $\frac{1}{4}$ [ ] %

0.75 [ ] % $\frac{7}{10}$ [ ] %   0.19 [ ] % $\frac{15}{5}$ [ ] %   0.44 [ ] %

$\frac{9}{4}$ [ ] %   0.29 [ ] % $\frac{6}{12}$ [ ] %   0.55 [ ] % $\frac{1}{100}$ [ ] %

0.17 [ ] % $\frac{2}{100}$ [ ] %   2.5 [ ] % $\frac{5}{20}$ [ ] %   0.50 [ ] %

$\frac{8}{10}$ [ ] %   0.42 [ ] % $\frac{15}{20}$ [ ] % $\frac{1}{5}$ [ ] %   0.06 [ ] %

Started: Finished: Total Time: Completed: Correct:

Answer Key

Unit 1: Addition

Test 1 Addition (page 12)

5	5	7	9
2	4	6	8
7	3	5	5
10	9	10	9
6	10	8	8

Test 2 Addition (page 13)

10	10	5	7
10	5	7	10
9	9	4	4
7	8	9	10
6	9	10	6

Test 3 Addition (page 14)

7	6	8	5
10	8	10	4
9	10	5	8
5	9	3	7
9	7	8	10

Test 4 Addition (page 15)

7	7	9	10
4	5	10	10
8	5	7	8
9	10	9	10
8	6	10	9

Test 5 Addition (page 16)

10	5	5	7	9
0	2	4	6	8
7	7	6	7	8
4	9	3	5	5
10	9	10	10	9
6	8	9	8	8

Test 6 Addition (page 17)

8	10	10	5	7
6	10	5	7	10
4	9	9	6	4
2	8	6	10	9
10	7	8	9	10
0	3	9	10	9

Test 7 Addition (page 18)

9	10	10	5	8
10	8	4	10	4
7	6	6	8	5
9	8	8	10	6
9	9	7	8	10
5	7	8	7	7

Test 8 Addition (page 19)

7	5	7	8	8
10	10	8	10	4
9	10	9	9	10
6	7	9	7	10
4	5	10	6	8
8	6	10	5	9

Test 9 Addition (page 20)

11	15	18	12
11	17	11	12
16	11	11	16
14	14	11	14
11	13	12	15

Test 10 Addition (page 21)

14	13	13	15
18	13	12	12
12	11	12	11
14	14	11	15
13	11	13	15

Test 11 Addition (page 22)

13	11	12	12
13	15	14	14
14	13	17	14
13	11	12	15
12	18	16	11

Test 12 Addition (page 23)

13	18	12	11
16	15	17	13
12	15	12	14
12	14	13	16
14	16	14	15

Test 13 Addition (page 24)

11	11	12	12	11
12	14	13	16	14
14	16	13	11	17
12	13	16	18	13
12	15	14	12	13
15	11	11	13	15

Test 14 Addition (page 25)

11	14	12	13	13
13	11	16	16	11
12	17	11	11	13
15	12	11	15	15
14	13	18	12	16
15	14	11	17	12

Test 15 Addition (page 26)

15	14	16	18	15
11	13	14	18	14
12	17	13	15	16
13	12	11	12	13
12	17	16	16	11
13	12	11	12	11

Test 16 Addition (page 27)

17	17	11	15	13
12	13	18	13	12
16	13	15	12	13
12	16	12	14	11
12	11	14	13	16
14	16	14	17	14

Test 17 Addition (page 28)

14	11	11	11
12	12	13	14
18	17	20	15
14	15	16	13
20	15	13	18

Test 18 Addition (page 29)

16	15	18	12
11	16	11	12
16	11	13	14
14	20	11	14
19	13	12	15

Test 19 Addition (page 30)

19	13	15	14	13
12	16	12	14	11
17	17	12	15	13
20	13	18	13	11
12	12	14	13	16
12	16	12	17	14

Test 20 Addition (page 31)

20	11	14	13	16
14	13	19	12	14
15	18	11	17	12
12	17	13	15	16
13	12	12	11	13
14	16	12	17	14

Test 21 Addition (page 32)

4	8	12	9
5	9	13	10
12	5	12	15
9	17	11	4
9	7	14	10

Answer Key *(cont.)*

Unit 1: Addition *(cont.)*

Test 22 Addition (page 33)

5	9	13	10
11	16	11	4
10	3	10	13
7	10	9	2
8	6	18	8

Test 23 Addition (page 34)

12	5	12	14
9	12	11	4
12	8	10	10
7	11	15	17
13	5	13	16

Test 24 Addition (page 35)

6	16	10	11
14	18	8	16
16	13	19	9
12	14	13	11
10	16	17	9

Test 25 Addition (page 36)

19	17	6	15	12
10	6	10	13	15
8	8	15	5	11
7	8	6	9	11
12	10	8	13	10
18	17	14	11	9

Test 26 Addition (page 37)

13	6	10	4	8
19	14	6	10	12
8	6	16	5	11
17	9	8	14	10
18	17	14	11	14
20	8	6	9	11

Test 27 Addition (page 38)

10	5	11	7	13
9	17	8	6	11
15	7	16	13	18
19	9	11	9	14
12	15	10	12	12
20	9	10	7	13

Test 28 Addition (page 39)

7	9	8	9	15
10	19	5	16	10
8	8	9	12	8
7	13	13	10	9
10	4	11	6	17
18	8	7	12	13

Test 29 Addition (page 40)

9	8	9	12	8
9	13	9	5	8
17	8	4	12	4
9	6	12	11	9
15	8	18	10	6
9	10	7	16	9
10	10	16	6	3
20	14	12	14	5

Test 30 Addition (page 41)

19	15	2	16	18
9	11	16	13	11
11	9	13	14	11
17	9	17	13	15
7	12	15	16	12
12	8	12	8	19
5	13	12	11	13
11	10	7	14	3

Test 31 Addition (page 42)

17	16	12	13	4
7	12	14	19	11
17	14	15	10	14
16	12	4	13	15
12	11	16	12	7
12	15	15	12	11
8	14	7	13	13
18	11	13	14	10

Test 32 Addition (page 43)

9	11	16	13	11
17	12	17	13	15
9	13	9	9	10
7	11	15	17	10
19	15	2	16	18
7	12	15	16	12
12	17	15	18	11
5	10	9	13	9

Test 33 Addition (page 44)

8	10	15	14	9
18	11	16	12	14
10	9	7	15	10
17	10	16	6	11
18	14	3	17	14
6	8	13	19	12
13	16	10	9	5
7	5	9	10	9
12	8	4	11	11
11	8	7	0	20

Test 34 Addition (page 45)

10	10	16	14	15
19	11	13	10	12
17	13	15	15	9
13	13	11	10	14
9	16	14	11	10
10	12	12	11	15
18	19	11	12	18
9	11	9	13	17
20	13	8	12	12
8	12	9	9	14

Test 35 Addition (page 46)

10	9	7	15	11
17	10	16	6	11
18	14	3	17	14
6	8	15	10	12
13	16	10	9	5
5	5	9	10	9
12	8	4	9	7
11	8	7	20	13
7	12	11	15	12
13	14	19	8	18

Test 36 Addition (page 47)

6	6	10	11	13
10	7	4	9	7
16	11	8	11	14
14	13	12	15	10
11	20	19	9	18
10	8	12	14	7
16	8	17	8	9
18	12	3	17	14
15	11	13	10	12
13	14	9	15	4

Unit 2: Subtraction

Test 1 Subtraction (page 48)

5	6	7	5
0	2	0	1
3	3	1	1
1	3	1	4
5	0	2	3

Test 2 Subtraction (page 49)

3	6	4	5
2	1	9	3
1	2	3	4
3	2	6	10
2	7	0	1

Test 3 Subtraction (page 50)

4	0	3	5
7	0	0	1
6	4	3	1
3	1	0	6
2	8	6	9

Test 4 Subtraction (page 51)

3	2	3	2
5	3	4	1
5	4	2	3
6	4	2	4
0	2	6	0

Test 5 Subtraction (page 52)

4	0	6	5	4
6	3	5	6	3
8	6	8	3	1
1	0	2	10	2
4	6	0	3	2
0	4	1	1	1

Test 6 Subtraction (page 53)

0	1	2	0	4
1	7	6	2	1
1	0	2	3	3
1	2	1	4	4
0	2	4	6	2
6	0	8	3	1

Test 7 Subtraction (page 54)

3	9	6	2	4
8	5	3	5	2
2	1	1	6	0
1	2	1	1	4
2	4	0	5	10
3	5	3	1	3

Test 8 Subtraction (page 55)

3	3	0	2	1
4	5	0	5	4
2	10	0	7	2
2	1	3	1	4
3	5	2	4	0
3	4	6	2	2

Test 9 Subtraction (page 56)

9	9	7	8
9	6	7	7
9	4	4	6
9	2	8	6
7	7	9	6

Test 10 Subtraction (page 57)

7	7	4	7
8	9	9	6
5	9	8	8
2	9	9	9
8	7	6	6

Test 11 Subtraction (page 58)

7	9	6	8
9	9	9	8
8	6	6	7
4	3	5	2
8	7	5	9

Test 12 Subtraction (page 59)

9	9	5	9
5	7	4	9
8	7	4	2
8	3	6	6
7	8	6	6

Test 13 Subtraction (page 60)

9	8	7	6	6
5	8	4	7	5
8	6	8	5	6
8	7	7	5	6
7	7	4	4	9
8	9	3	9	9

Test 14 Subtraction (page 61)

9	8	9	6	5
9	8	4	7	8
6	7	5	4	4
9	3	9	3	6
2	7	7	6	8
9	8	7	6	5

Test 15 Subtraction (page 62)

8	8	7	5	2
9	7	6	5	7
7	8	8	9	6
7	9	9	4	7
8	8	9	5	5
6	6	9	4	3

Test 16 Subtraction (page 63)

5	5	3	9	9
9	7	4	8	6
8	5	7	5	9
8	6	7	3	6
9	8	4	4	7
9	8	9	7	2

Test 17 Subtraction (page 64)

7	1	4	6
8	8	9	8
1	4	9	1
5	9	3	3
8	8	2	9

Test 18 Subtraction (page 65)

8	0	6	9
6	6	8	7
1	9	5	4
2	7	3	8
9	9	7	5

Test 19 Subtraction (page 66)

7	6	8	7
7	2	9	7
8	7	9	8
7	6	3	6
9	7	5	6

Test 20 Subtraction (page 67)

9	6	9	9
3	9	1	8
5	8	4	8
8	2	9	8
5	5	0	3

Test 21 Subtraction (page 68)

2	9	9	4	6
8	8	4	9	8
7	3	4	9	8
5	9	3	5	3
8	2	8	7	9
6	6	5	5	7

Answer Key (cont.)

Unit 2: Subtraction (cont.)

Test 22 Subtraction (page 69)

9	7	9	5	4
5	5	9	6	8
4	7	6	8	1
6	1	9	2	5
7	7	3	3	4
0	8	4	6	3

Test 23 Subtraction (page 70)

2	7	4	5	9
7	7	7	9	3
8	9	0	6	1
7	8	5	3	3
2	9	7	8	6
8	8	4	9	8

Test 24 Subtraction (page 71)

9	6	1	6	9
5	4	5	2	3
2	5	7	7	9
7	6	3	6	4
9	6	9	3	8
8	3	8	3	4

Test 25 Subtraction (page 72)

3	8	8	5	7
2	1	9	6	3
5	9	5	8	3
2	7	7	5	3
3	8	9	6	5
0	9	4	4	7

Test 26 Subtraction (page 73)

1	8	9	5	8
0	5	6	2	5
6	0	7	6	6
5	9	3	8	4
3	3	9	5	7
4	9	9	7	5
2	8	7	4	1
3	4	8	2	7

Test 27 Subtraction (page 74)

1	9	3	6	8
3	5	9	6	5
9	2	1	7	5
4	6	8	8	2
8	2	8	7	6
5	4	6	8	5
6	3	0	9	6
2	7	7	9	4

Test 28 Subtraction (page 75)

9	4	4	3	0
5	4	5	5	7
1	7	9	6	8
7	6	9	3	3
1	5	6	9	3
9	5	10	7	5
8	6	4	8	2
4	9	7	7	0

Test 29 Subtraction (page 76)

6	1	7	4	9
6	9	1	9	5
3	8	9	2	0
1	8	3	2	4
8	8	9	0	5
2	7	9	6	8
1	8	5	5	4
5	5	7	1	9

Test 30 Subtraction (page 77)

9	3	9	5	9
0	9	9	7	8
7	4	6	2	5
8	2	7	6	5
5	8	8	3	5
2	7	7	8	7
4	6	9	2	9
6	0	9	7	6

Test 31 Subtraction (page 78)

9	7	4	9	4
4	8	4	0	5
1	6	9	3	0
5	3	6	9	3
5	6	8	7	0
1	6	8	9	7
2	7	1	5	9
2	6	3	8	8
6	9	4	8	6
4	7	3	7	8

Test 32 Subtraction (page 79)

2	8	7	2	5
7	9	3	6	7
5	6	5	5	0
8	2	0	1	6
8	9	6	8	7
5	0	6	4	4
4	7	7	5	3
3	1	7	8	6
2	1	3	7	5
6	6	4	7	9

Test 33 Subtraction (page 80)

8	6	3	7	9
4	1	8	2	8
7	0	7	7	8
8	3	5	9	5
5	8	7	6	4
5	4	2	6	9
5	9	6	9	1
8	5	7	9	4
6	3	6	2	3
9	6	4	4	3

Test 34 Subtraction (page 81)

6	9	4	3	0
6	9	5	2	2
4	7	9	7	8
9	4	4	4	9
8	1	8	0	7
6	6	5	9	3
3	7	8	3	6
7	6	6	5	3
9	8	6	1	4
9	8	5	5	7

Test 35 Subtraction (page 82)

9	5	2	6	9
1	3	7	4	8
4	3	6	7	9
6	8	8	2	3
5	7	5	2	4
5	0	9	8	8
6	7	8	4	6
3	8	5	4	6
9	0	9	5	9
1	4	4	1	5

Test 36 Subtraction (page 83)

1	6	9	5	4
8	9	8	9	8
9	5	7	2	6
3	9	3	2	8
7	2	3	0	6
7	4	5	8	7
4	1	9	9	0
4	4	2	1	3
6	7	6	1	5
7	0	5	8	3

Answer Key *(cont.)*

Unit 3: Multiplication

Test 1 Multiplication (page 84)

0	2	6	4
8	10	1	3
4	12	5	8
7	16	0	14
6	18	0	9

Test 2 Multiplication (page 85)

0	8	6	21
18	18	7	0
5	12	0	15
6	16	4	24
4	9	27	0

Test 3 Multiplication (page 86)

0	1	27	6	2
0	10	15	3	8
0	6	14	21	9
4	5	8	0	12
12	0	16	18	0
0	7	4	2	24

Test 4 Multiplication (page 87)

2	2	10	0	4
6	0	7	16	9
14	27	12	9	0
3	5	15	0	18
6	24	4	8	12
0	8	6	21	0

Test 5 Multiplication (page 88)

20	12	12	5
7	16	9	28
24	27	14	9
0	16	36	6
18	8	32	21

Test 6 Multiplication (page 89)

15	20	8	6	10
0	14	24	12	21
28	18	18	7	9
5	8	0	32	0
12	6	16	27	12
24	16	3	9	0

Test 7 Multiplication (page 90)

10	21	32	8
16	25	15	3
35	20	24	18
36	30	16	8
28	40	14	0

Test 8 Multiplication (page 91)

12	7	16	9	35
10	12	9	0	27
28	15	4	18	20
24	4	6	16	40
30	6	24	0	25
21	45	8	5	8

Test 9 Multiplication (page 92)

12	24	36	48
7	21	35	49
6	18	30	42
14	28	42	56
0	54	0	63

Test 10 Multiplication (page 93)

48	72	36	12
35	21	49	42
16	48	32	64
18	28	63	14
0	8	24	40

Test 11 Multiplication (page 94)

30	28	24	14
16	18	56	40
48	32	24	42
35	36	8	12
48	21	49	56

Test 12 Multiplication (page 95)

35	45	7	32
16	36	21	40
63	54	49	72
28	24	56	27
42	56	14	72

Test 13 Multiplication (page 96)

24	18	28	64
35	81	42	56
63	54	63	36
56	45	49	8
14	40	48	32

Test 14 Multiplication (page 97)

60	24	70	55
66	36	77	96
10	99	33	108
22	90	48	30
72	80	44	50

Test 15 Multiplication (page 98)

66	20	77	120
72	33	84	80
70	99	36	108
24	90	48	30
72	88	40	132

Test 16 Multiplication (page 99)

120	12	121	60
50	22	96	44
110	11	20	132
100	144	48	55
110	40	84	88

Test 17 Multiplication (page 100)

6	18	7	45
30	15	56	32
21	9	24	18
10	27	8	0
12	72	32	45

Test 18 Multiplication (page 101)

24	18	28	64
35	81	42	56
63	54	63	36
56	45	49	8
16	40	48	27

Test 19 Multiplication (page 102)

14	8	18	64
24	81	30	12
35	28	45	24
20	8	21	18
56	36	48	54

Test 20 Multiplication (page 103)

24	18	8	40
35	72	42	21
27	30	63	36
56	45	36	8
32	12	28	56

Test 21 Multiplication (page 104)

24	42	24	27	45
25	40	48	63	42
16	28	15	3	56
30	15	49	36	18
20	28	0	48	72
12	8	63	81	30

Answer Key (cont.)

Unit 3: Multiplication (cont.)

Test 22 Multiplication (page 105)

1	18	12	12	25
36	35	64	81	14
6	16	30	18	49
40	45	8	8	21
32	35	12	21	0
72	4	40	24	63

Test 23 Multiplication (page 106)

16	30	32	0	20
42	48	12	72	28
42	12	35	28	56
36	7	72	54	48
18	24	6	24	63
16	27	63	24	6

Test 24 Multiplication (page 107)

5	20	27	72	32
12	8	48	40	49
35	10	15	4	54
30	14	72	36	15
0	9	9	45	21
4	27	10	24	40

Test 25 Multiplication (page 108)

42	14	16	25	24
40	5	63	36	9
30	48	15	72	42
48	64	35	4	27
21	35	6	54	0
21	36	10	15	28

Test 26 Multiplication (page 109)

12	28	32	18	12
18	42	48	9	30
6	12	30	18	49
40	20	32	45	9
24	40	0	21	0
27	4	15	24	35
6	8	12	8	10
56	63	3	81	16

Test 27 Multiplication (page 110)

18	35	48	27	14
24	32	56	18	14
9	16	25	36	49
24	35	32	45	15
28	8	12	8	10
64	63	3	81	48
12	40	12	21	0
54	0	20	24	28

Test 28 Multiplication (page 111)

42	56	24	81	16
15	28	54	9	30
6	12	20	18	63
16	30	32	36	21
20	45	36	21	0
27	4	40	24	0
40	45	6	18	10
9	6	72	36	8

Test 29 Multiplication (page 112)

20	32	28	4	14
24	35	32	45	15
18	21	16	63	14
18	10	64	12	5
9	16	25	36	49
28	8	12	8	10
12	30	12	20	0
40	30	24	36	16

Test 30 Multiplication (page 113)

18	20	45	24	42
0	6	24	30	56
27	32	10	48	56
54	0	30	12	28
0	10	36	16	16
9	28	25	12	21
81	6	35	36	35
12	16	40	18	49

Test 31 Multiplication (page 114)

15	32	15	42	24
12	28	32	18	12
30	18	56	48	9
21	8	30	36	21
40	20	12	45	9
24	40	24	49	0
45	0	35	18	35
36	18	12	10	16
56	63	3	81	16
27	42	64	7	24

Test 32 Multiplication (page 115)

24	20	40	18	21
48	14	32	27	4
54	6	63	30	0
27	28	25	36	42
24	15	16	54	15
36	30	24	28	0
48	9	20	42	21
45	8	12	16	8
40	63	6	81	18
64	14	12	0	72

Test 33 Multiplication (page 116)

10	32	15	20	27
15	32	30	42	24
6	24	28	16	54
30	18	56	48	9
35	48	9	16	36
24	40	18	49	0
27	20	0	35	36
21	6	28	25	21
45	18	12	10	12
3	42	64	81	18

Test 34 Multiplication (page 117)

6	24	25	48	9
8	63	8	81	12
30	18	56	54	9
21	16	30	36	14
40	20	12	45	24
28	40	12	49	0
45	4	35	0	35
36	14	8	10	36
72	63	3	18	16
27	42	64	0	32

Test 35 Multiplication (page 118)

40	72	0	63	16
18	28	64	54	14
24	20	30	54	49
10	20	32	45	9
24	40	12	21	0
15	4	35	24	21
6	8	12	8	25
36	28	15	42	56
18	35	48	42	30
27	24	36	9	18

Test 36 Multiplication (page 119)

27	16	36	8	27
18	28	24	54	12
18	10	16	0	6
32	63	5	81	4
48	21	14	4	36
30	16	12	25	12
24	28	15	42	56
54	40	36	6	10
18	32	30	48	49
35	64	24	45	9

Answer Key (cont.)

Unit 4: Division

Test 1 Division (page 120)

5	5
3	4
1	4
4	5
6	1
4	3
7	5
7	2
4	10
9	8

Test 2 Division (page 121)

8	8	3	7
3	5	5	9
1	2	2	1
4	7	9	9
4	4	10	7

Test 3 Division (page 122)

4	6
5	6
9	10
2	5
2	2
7	3
8	2
5	3
3	6
4	1

Test 4 Division (page 123)

3	8	7	5
5	6	6	3
8	6	8	4
4	7	4	8
5	4	5	3

Test 5 Division (page 124)

2	7	4
3	8	1
3	9	2
2	3	4
7	6	4
5	9	7
3	8	7
4	5	1
8	5	5
6	5	4

Test 6 Division (page 125)

2	6	4	3	2
8	9	3	5	8
8	6	6	1	4
7	6	5	7	7
4	9	2	3	1
5	8	9	9	3

Test 7 Division (page 126)

1	6	4
2	4	1
3	4	5
3	1	6
8	2	7
1	6	4
5	2	1
6	8	7
4	8	5
2	3	7

Test 8 Division (page 127)

1	5	1	8	9
3	6	3	7	4
4	5	2	9	7
4	6	3	9	4
4	9	2	5	2
5	6	8	7	6

Test 9 Division (page 128)

3	8
0	2
3	5
3	4
8	0
4	1
4	9
5	7
2	1
6	2

Test 10 Division (page 129)

2	1	7	1
5	8	3	5
3	2	6	0
3	6	9	7
3	1	4	4

Test 11 Division (page 130)

5	6
8	2
9	9
2	1
5	6
8	7
4	4
9	3
5	8
4	7

Test 12 Division (page 131)

7	3	9	3
4	2	6	1
4	9	0	4
8	3	1	9
8	2	2	6

Test 13 Division (page 132)

2	4	4
6	6	9
8	2	2
7	3	5
4	6	4
2	9	7
1	8	3
3	7	7
9	3	5
1	5	8

Test 14 Division (page 133)

5	5	7	8	5
8	6	6	8	1
7	3	4	9	3
4	8	9	7	4
6	3	3	1	9
2	2	2	2	5

Test 15 Division (page 134)

3	1	3
6	2	1
5	3	4
5	8	9
9	9	6
4	4	4
7	6	8
5	7	6
7	3	2
2	8	5

Answer Key *(cont.)*

Unit 4: Division *(cont.)*

Test 16 Division (page 135)

2	1	3	9	7
1	9	1	3	6
2	7	5	1	5
3	3	9	7	3
2	9	4	5	8
4	5	8	8	2

Test 17 Division (page 136)

4	4
6	6
6	8
4	3
2	9
5	7
8	9
9	8
6	9
9	8

Test 18 Division (page 137)

4	8	6	9
7	5	4	10
5	7	6	3
7	5	5	3
4	4	8	9

Test 19 Division (page 138)

7	9
7	8
6	8
8	5
6	3
6	3
6	9
9	9
6	3
7	9

Test 20 Division (page 139)

6	9	8	9
6	8	9	4
4	7	9	6
2	4	9	3
8	7	7	7

Test 21 Division (page 140)

3	9	3
9	6	7
4	9	7
4	6	6
4	3	6
5	7	9
6	4	5
5	5	5
6	2	7
3	7	2

Test 22 Division (page 141)

6	3	4	3	5
6	8	8	7	8
7	8	6	9	2
4	2	5	5	6
2	2	9	7	6
2	3	5	5	8

Test 23 Division (page 142)

3	3	5
3	6	7
3	9	6
8	8	8
9	6	2
3	8	7
5	2	9
2	5	9
5	9	4
7	5	8

Test 24 Division (page 143)

3	5	9	4	7
4	2	9	8	4
3	4	3	4	6
7	6	6	5	8
6	1	2	5	3
6	7	9	6	6

Test 25 Division (page 144)

3	5	4
4	7	3
3	5	3
6	2	2
4	6	3
3	9	3
9	6	6
9	8	9
6	6	8
8	2	5

Test 26 Division (page 145)

4	2	9	8	4
9	4	5	5	8
6	8	8	7	8
7	4	9	9	4
8	9	4	9	3
4	2	9	6	9
5	6	5	2	7
7	5	2	3	6

Test 27 Division (page 146)

2	1	4	5	9
7	8	6	9	2
3	4	3	4	6
5	6	8	5	3
2	3	3	6	7
6	3	8	6	7
7	6	4	7	7
4	8	9	8	2

Test 28 Division (page 147)

4	8	8	9	6
2	3	3	9	2
7	6	8	9	3
4	9	2	7	5
4	5	8	7	9
3	7	5	5	4
8	2	6	2	4
5	7	4	9	8

Test 29 Division (page 148)

4	2	9	7	6
2	5	8	6	5
9	1	6	7	5
5	5	3	8	4
9	2	1	4	8
3	3	6	7	3
5	3	7	6	9
5	6	6	1	9

Test 30 Division (page 149)

3	4	4	4	7
2	3	5	8	3
5	8	6	5	5
6	7	9	6	7
5	3	9	9	3
1	4	8	9	7
4	4	8	6	7
7	6	6	5	8
2	2	3	2	7
9	4	3	7	8

Answer Key *(cont.)*

Unit 4: Division *(cont.)*

Test 31 Division (page 150)

3	3	4	8	7
5	1	4	7	6
4	6	8	5	4
9	7	7	9	8
1	9	9	9	4
9	1	4	6	9
1	2	5	6	5
4	8	6	7	7
8	2	2	5	9
2	6	3	5	5

Test 32 Division (page 151)

4	6	6	5	7
3	7	2	2	1
9	1	2	7	9
8	4	6	6	5
3	2	3	5	8
1	3	5	6	5
4	3	5	9	7
9	8	8	4	8
2	2	8	7	6
4	1	6	8	6

Test 33 Division (page 152)

2	6	8	3	7
5	3	2	5	1
8	9	8	3	6
9	2	3	9	3
6	7	7	3	8
4	5	4	5	7
5	3	6	5	4
5	8	7	1	6
7	2	3	7	6
6	3	7	8	9

Test 34 Division (page 153)

3	6	4	6
5	5	3	4
7	5	8	8
9	7	2	10
2	2	3	12

Test 35 Division (page 154)

1	4
6	12
2	5
7	6
7	3
7	8
4	2
9	3
5	11
4	12

Test 36 Division (page 155)

3	2	7	11
5	5	4	9
6	6	5	10
2	6	8	8
1	9	4	12

Unit 5: Mixed Math Facts

Test 1 Mixed Math Facts (page 156)

7	9	0	5
21	9	7	8
13	9	9	32
3	10	48	4
10	6	6	36

Test 2 Mixed Math Facts (page 157)

10	8	8	40
9	24	3	7
12	9	9	10
13	3	9	24
9	27	56	10

Test 3 Mixed Math Facts (page 158)

9	7	6	5
4	16	12	16
12	9	7	30
6	12	10	9
54	7	8	11

Test 4 Mixed Math Facts (page 159)

6	28	6	14
9	3	12	0
21	8	4	12
13	3	9	24
4	27	15	0

Test 5 Mixed Math Facts (page 160)

42	8	6	9
11	4	6	36
5	48	1	8
11	81	2	9
9	1	54	7

Test 6 Mixed Math Facts (page 161)

14	4	6	35	8
5	40	8	6	4
81	11	2	7	45
25	13	4	5	16
13	3	9	48	8
4	30	2	12	7

Test 7 Mixed Math Facts (page 162)

20	13	9	4	18
15	1	9	64	6
7	63	5	12	36
49	9	45	4	15
14	24	11	14	7
8	81	11	2	16

Answer Key *(cont.)*

Unit 5: Mixed Math Facts *(cont.)*

Test 8 Mixed Math Facts (page 163)

5	17	9	16	5
9	5	12	5	72
8	18	9	7	5
35	7	7	2	14
15	6	8	36	10
7	11	7	18	9

Test 9 Mixed Math Facts (page 164)

10	3	3	24	56
7	42	8	10	6
12	12	3	80	5
30	13	12	3	16
9	2	17	7	49
8	7	40	14	9

Test 10 Mixed Math Facts (page 165)

9	12	5	36	5
4	16	12	14	18
24	13	9	7	30
6	8	12	20	9
54	7	7	13	56
11	1	21	5	16

Test 11 Mixed Math Facts (page 166)

10	8	48	11	3
10	42	9	8	6
3	11	4	9	36
3	48	9	8	3
24	9	11	9	2
9	1	54	6	72
8	42	8	11	6
16	6	21	9	14

Test 12 Mixed Math Facts (page 167)

13	3	9	48	8
18	16	3	81	12
9	6	28	27	14
6	13	8	9	24
6	9	3	12	0
21	3	8	4	15
4	30	2	11	7
4	21	15	3	0

Test 13 Mixed Math Facts (page 168)

5	10	8	4	40
7	9	24	3	9
42	12	9	9	9
4	36	13	5	4
7	14	5	7	15
6	9	54	56	10
16	6	11	8	32
10	12	6	30	10

Test 14 Mixed Math Facts (page 169)

2	12	0	4	11
5	7	12	0	4
4	14	9	7	8
14	9	9	36	6
10	12	3	48	4
10	6	6	36	7
18	7	11	42	8
17	3	45	8	1

Test 15 Mixed Math Facts (page 170)

7	18	15	5	7
12	3	7	21	4
3	4	15	10	10
8	15	20	6	9
3	4	14	25	49
63	2	5	4	13
11	6	28	27	15
12	8	9	24	7

Test 16 Mixed Math Facts (page 171)

9	9	72	9	12
8	7	40	14	8
4	9	9	54	7
11	4	8	18	11
42	14	4	9	12
9	8	2	17	35
6	3	21	12	6
10	24	7	5	6
7	2	13	2	56
36	7	64	4	16

Test 17 Mixed Math Facts (page 172)

21	7	11	14	4
25	15	3	5	64
9	4	16	12	16
9	14	4	5	32
5	12	8	27	6
3	28	18	49	7
13	6	14	48	7
8	3	12	3	15
8	6	3	54	7
16	7	18	9	9

Test 18 Mixed Math Facts (page 173)

36	7	5	10	27
1	8	42	5	18
12	2	6	48	5
11	4	7	35	2
3	60	3	9	2
9	8	35	8	7
72	12	0	6	54
20	14	5	6	15
12	4	11	32	7
6	24	3	10	7

Test 19 Mixed Math Facts (page 174)

7	14	30	3	5	13
6	42	16	2	90	4
7	20	12	9	4	18
4	5	63	5	12	36
3	10	3	2	24	72
54	8	24	8	10	6
8	15	1	7	64	6
4	49	3	45	4	15
2	11	24	9	14	7
32	9	81	11	2	16

Test 20 Mixed Math Facts (page 175)

7	8	10	6	6	36
9	5	17	9	16	5
1	9	5	12	4	72
49	8	18	9	7	5
4	35	13	7	2	14
6	42	4	40	3	14
8	15	6	8	27	10
9	8	14	7	18	9
12	18	6	48	5	14
7	27	8	7	12	4

Answer Key (cont.)

Unit 6: Fractions

Test 1 Fractions (page 176)

$\frac{1}{2}$	$\frac{1}{3}$	$\frac{1}{2}$	$\frac{1}{3}$
$\frac{2}{3}$	$\frac{1}{2}$	$\frac{3}{4}$	$\frac{1}{2}$
$\frac{1}{4}$	$\frac{1}{3}$	$\frac{1}{3}$	$\frac{1}{2}$
$\frac{1}{5}$	$\frac{1}{2}$	$\frac{1}{5}$	$\frac{2}{3}$
$\frac{3}{4}$	1	$\frac{1}{2}$	$\frac{4}{7}$

Test 2 Fractions (page 177)

$\frac{1}{4}$	$\frac{1}{7}$	$\frac{3}{4}$	$\frac{4}{5}$
$\frac{1}{3}$	$\frac{1}{2}$	$\frac{1}{2}$	$\frac{1}{4}$
$\frac{1}{3}$	$\frac{2}{3}$	$\frac{2}{5}$	$\frac{1}{6}$
$\frac{2}{3}$	$\frac{1}{5}$	$\frac{1}{2}$	$\frac{1}{4}$
$\frac{1}{6}$	$\frac{1}{3}$	$\frac{1}{2}$	$\frac{1}{10}$

Test 3 Fractions (page 178)

$\frac{1}{2}$	$\frac{1}{2}$	$\frac{1}{4}$	$\frac{1}{3}$	$\frac{1}{3}$
$\frac{1}{2}$	$\frac{1}{2}$	$\frac{1}{3}$	$\frac{1}{2}$	$\frac{1}{3}$
$\frac{1}{2}$	$\frac{1}{7}$	$\frac{5}{7}$	$\frac{1}{4}$	$\frac{1}{4}$
$\frac{1}{2}$	$\frac{7}{8}$	$\frac{1}{6}$	$\frac{1}{5}$	$\frac{1}{5}$
$\frac{1}{8}$	$\frac{1}{3}$	$\frac{1}{7}$	1	$\frac{1}{2}$
1	$\frac{1}{4}$	$\frac{1}{6}$	$\frac{1}{4}$	$\frac{1}{3}$

Test 4 Fractions (page 179)

$\frac{1}{4}$	$\frac{1}{2}$	$\frac{3}{5}$	$\frac{1}{11}$	$\frac{3}{4}$
$\frac{1}{3}$	$\frac{1}{7}$	$\frac{1}{3}$	$\frac{1}{8}$	$\frac{1}{8}$
$\frac{1}{2}$	$\frac{1}{9}$	$\frac{1}{10}$	$\frac{1}{4}$	1
1	$\frac{1}{3}$	$\frac{1}{2}$	$\frac{2}{3}$	1
$\frac{1}{6}$	$\frac{1}{3}$	$\frac{1}{3}$	$\frac{1}{2}$	$\frac{1}{2}$
$\frac{1}{4}$	$\frac{1}{6}$	$\frac{2}{3}$	$\frac{1}{11}$	$\frac{1}{7}$

Test 5 Fractions (page 180)

$\frac{3}{4}$	$\frac{1}{11}$	$\frac{1}{5}$	$\frac{1}{2}$	$\frac{1}{5}$
$\frac{1}{6}$	$\frac{1}{10}$	1	$\frac{1}{11}$	$\frac{1}{3}$
$\frac{1}{7}$	$\frac{1}{4}$	$\frac{1}{11}$	$\frac{1}{5}$	$\frac{1}{6}$
$\frac{1}{9}$	$\frac{1}{4}$	$\frac{2}{3}$	$\frac{1}{5}$	$\frac{1}{6}$
$\frac{1}{2}$	$\frac{1}{8}$	$\frac{1}{3}$	$\frac{1}{3}$	1
$\frac{1}{3}$	$\frac{1}{2}$	$\frac{2}{3}$	$\frac{1}{12}$	$\frac{1}{2}$
$\frac{4}{7}$	$\frac{1}{2}$	$\frac{2}{5}$	$\frac{1}{8}$	$\frac{1}{2}$
$\frac{5}{6}$	$\frac{1}{4}$	$\frac{4}{5}$	$\frac{1}{4}$	$\frac{5}{7}$

Test 6 Fractions (page 181)

$\frac{1}{3}$	$\frac{1}{12}$	$\frac{1}{4}$	$\frac{1}{10}$	$\frac{5}{7}$
$\frac{1}{2}$	$\frac{1}{6}$	$\frac{1}{7}$	$\frac{1}{11}$	$\frac{3}{5}$
$\frac{1}{6}$	$\frac{1}{3}$	$\frac{1}{3}$	1	$\frac{1}{2}$
$\frac{2}{3}$	$\frac{1}{8}$	$\frac{1}{5}$	$\frac{1}{3}$	$\frac{1}{3}$
1	$\frac{3}{7}$	$\frac{1}{8}$	$\frac{1}{4}$	$\frac{9}{10}$
$\frac{1}{12}$	1	$\frac{1}{9}$	$\frac{1}{12}$	$\frac{2}{15}$
$\frac{1}{6}$	$\frac{4}{7}$	$\frac{1}{11}$	$\frac{1}{9}$	$\frac{9}{10}$
$\frac{4}{5}$	$\frac{3}{7}$	$\frac{3}{4}$	$\frac{4}{9}$	$\frac{2}{5}$

Test 7 Fractions (page 182)

3	$1\frac{2}{3}$	4	$1\frac{1}{2}$
$1\frac{1}{4}$	$1\frac{3}{5}$	$1\frac{1}{3}$	$1\frac{1}{4}$
3	$1\frac{1}{7}$	$2\frac{1}{6}$	$1\frac{2}{5}$
$2\frac{2}{3}$	$2\frac{1}{3}$	3	$3\frac{2}{5}$
$1\frac{1}{2}$	$3\frac{3}{4}$	5	7

Test 8 Fractions (page 183)

5	$1\frac{2}{3}$	4	2
$1\frac{2}{7}$	$3\frac{1}{2}$	$3\frac{1}{3}$	3
5	$1\frac{3}{4}$	2	$2\frac{1}{2}$
8	4	$4\frac{2}{5}$	$2\frac{1}{7}$
$2\frac{1}{2}$	$1\frac{1}{3}$	6	$1\frac{1}{2}$

Test 9 Fractions (page 184)

$1\frac{7}{12}$	$1\frac{1}{2}$	$1\frac{1}{2}$	5	$1\frac{3}{7}$
$1\frac{3}{4}$	$1\frac{1}{2}$	$3\frac{1}{3}$	7	$5\frac{1}{2}$
$1\frac{1}{8}$	$2\frac{1}{7}$	3	$2\frac{5}{6}$	$1\frac{1}{5}$
$1\frac{1}{12}$	2	$2\frac{2}{3}$	$1\frac{1}{8}$	$1\frac{2}{3}$
$1\frac{1}{3}$	$1\frac{1}{2}$	2	$1\frac{2}{3}$	4
$1\frac{1}{3}$	$1\frac{1}{2}$	$1\frac{1}{7}$	$1\frac{3}{4}$	2

Test 10 Fractions (page 185)

3	$1\frac{1}{4}$	$1\frac{1}{2}$	$2\frac{1}{3}$	5
$1\frac{1}{6}$	3	4	$1\frac{1}{2}$	$6\frac{1}{4}$
$1\frac{1}{8}$	2	3	$3\frac{2}{7}$	$1\frac{4}{5}$
$2\frac{1}{9}$	4	$3\frac{1}{6}$	3	4
$4\frac{2}{3}$	$3\frac{2}{5}$	2	4	8
$3\frac{1}{3}$	$2\frac{1}{4}$	$3\frac{1}{5}$	5	$6\frac{2}{5}$

Test 11 Fractions (page 186)

$1\frac{1}{2}$	4	$2\frac{2}{3}$	$3\frac{3}{10}$	4
$2\frac{1}{2}$	$2\frac{2}{3}$	4	$1\frac{4}{5}$	$1\frac{1}{10}$
2	5	$2\frac{2}{5}$	6	$1\frac{2}{7}$
5	3	5	$1\frac{3}{7}$	$1\frac{1}{6}$
4	$1\frac{1}{2}$	3	8	2
$1\frac{4}{5}$	5	7	$1\frac{3}{5}$	2
6	$3\frac{1}{2}$	2	4	$1\frac{1}{2}$
$2\frac{1}{2}$	2	$1\frac{2}{3}$	$5\frac{1}{3}$	2

Test 12 Fractions (page 187)

2	$1\frac{3}{7}$	$1\frac{1}{2}$	$1\frac{3}{4}$	$1\frac{1}{2}$
2	$2\frac{2}{3}$	3	6	3
7	4	$1\frac{2}{3}$	$1\frac{3}{8}$	$1\frac{1}{4}$
4	3	$2\frac{1}{4}$	$2\frac{1}{2}$	2
$1\frac{3}{5}$	$1\frac{1}{6}$	$1\frac{1}{7}$	$1\frac{2}{5}$	$2\frac{2}{3}$
$1\frac{1}{2}$	4	$1\frac{1}{2}$	3	$1\frac{1}{3}$
2	$1\frac{1}{6}$	$1\frac{1}{4}$	5	2
2	4	$1\frac{3}{5}$	$2\frac{1}{5}$	2

Test 13 Fractions (page 188)

$\frac{2}{5}$	$1\frac{2}{3}$	$1\frac{4}{7}$	$\frac{5}{11}$
$\frac{1}{6}$	$3\frac{1}{2}$	$\frac{1}{2}$	$2\frac{2}{5}$
$5\frac{1}{4}$	4	$\frac{5}{6}$	$\frac{1}{2}$
$\frac{2}{5}$	5	$\frac{1}{3}$	$\frac{1}{4}$
8	$\frac{3}{7}$	$8\frac{1}{4}$	$4\frac{1}{2}$

Test 14 Fractions (page 189)

$2\frac{3}{4}$	$\frac{1}{3}$	$1\frac{1}{4}$	$2\frac{4}{5}$
$\frac{2}{5}$	6	$1\frac{4}{5}$	$\frac{1}{5}$
2	$\frac{1}{3}$	4	$2\frac{1}{5}$
$\frac{1}{6}$	2	$\frac{3}{5}$	3
$3\frac{1}{5}$	$\frac{1}{3}$	6	$\frac{1}{3}$

Test 15 Fractions (page 190)

7	$\frac{3}{4}$	$1\frac{2}{9}$	$\frac{5}{9}$	2
$3\frac{1}{2}$	$\frac{1}{2}$	$1\frac{1}{2}$	$\frac{1}{6}$	$\frac{1}{3}$
$\frac{1}{3}$	$1\frac{1}{3}$	3	$\frac{1}{3}$	$\frac{1}{9}$
$\frac{3}{8}$	1	2	$2\frac{1}{7}$	8
6	5	$4\frac{1}{2}$	2	$\frac{7}{9}$
9	$\frac{1}{2}$	$1\frac{3}{10}$	$\frac{9}{10}$	3

Test 16 Fractions (page 191)

7	$\frac{3}{5}$	$\frac{2}{3}$	$2\frac{2}{3}$	1
$\frac{1}{4}$	$4\frac{1}{2}$	$\frac{1}{2}$	$\frac{1}{3}$	7
2	$\frac{1}{5}$	2	$1\frac{1}{5}$	4
3	$\frac{2}{3}$	$10\frac{1}{2}$	$5\frac{1}{3}$	$\frac{1}{3}$
3	6	11	$1\frac{1}{3}$	$\frac{7}{12}$
$1\frac{1}{2}$	$\frac{1}{4}$	$3\frac{3}{10}$	$\frac{1}{2}$	$\frac{1}{9}$

Test 17 Fractions (page 192)

1	4	3	3	9
$\frac{1}{2}$	$3\frac{1}{3}$	$1\frac{2}{7}$	$1\frac{1}{2}$	2
4	$\frac{3}{4}$	$\frac{1}{8}$	5	$\frac{1}{10}$
$1\frac{2}{5}$	9	$\frac{1}{3}$	4	$1\frac{1}{4}$
$\frac{1}{3}$	$\frac{1}{2}$	$\frac{2}{3}$	$\frac{1}{4}$	4
2	$2\frac{1}{2}$	2	$\frac{1}{5}$	2
$\frac{5}{6}$	$\frac{2}{3}$	$3\frac{3}{5}$	$1\frac{5}{7}$	$\frac{1}{2}$
2	$\frac{4}{9}$	$\frac{1}{9}$	$1\frac{2}{3}$	1

Test 18 Fractions (page 193)

$3\frac{2}{3}$	$1\frac{1}{3}$	$3\frac{3}{4}$	2	$\frac{1}{6}$
$\frac{1}{3}$	1	2	$\frac{8}{9}$	$2\frac{2}{3}$
$2\frac{1}{5}$	$\frac{1}{4}$	$\frac{5}{7}$	$2\frac{1}{3}$	$\frac{1}{4}$
$1\frac{3}{4}$	$\frac{1}{5}$	2	$\frac{1}{6}$	8
$\frac{1}{5}$	6	$1\frac{1}{5}$	$\frac{5}{6}$	$\frac{1}{2}$
$1\frac{1}{4}$	$\frac{7}{8}$	$\frac{1}{10}$	4	4
$\frac{5}{9}$	3	$1\frac{1}{6}$	$1\frac{7}{8}$	1
6	$1\frac{1}{2}$	$\frac{7}{8}$	$1\frac{1}{14}$	$1\frac{1}{4}$

Unit 7: Fraction, Decimal, and Percent Equivalents

Test 1 Fraction Equivalents (page 194)

$\frac{1}{4}$	$\frac{1}{10}$	$\frac{1}{2}$	$\frac{7}{10}$
$\frac{1}{20}$	$\frac{9}{10}$	$\frac{1}{5}$	$\frac{9}{100}$
$\frac{1}{5}$	$1\frac{1}{2}$	$\frac{3}{20}$	$\frac{3}{4}$
$\frac{3}{20}$	$\frac{3}{5}$	$\frac{2}{5}$	$2\frac{3}{4}$
$\frac{7}{10}$	$\frac{3}{10}$	$\frac{11}{20}$	2

Test 2 Fraction Equivalents (page 195)

1	$\frac{1}{100}$	$\frac{4}{25}$	$\frac{33}{100}$
$\frac{7}{100}$	$\frac{4}{5}$	$2\frac{1}{4}$	3
$\frac{1}{5}$	$\frac{1}{2}$	$\frac{9}{10}$	$2\frac{1}{2}$
$1\frac{3}{4}$	$\frac{2}{5}$	$\frac{1}{200}$	$1\frac{1}{2}$
$\frac{3}{4}$	$\frac{9}{10}$	$\frac{1}{10}$	$1\frac{1}{2}$

Test 3 Fraction Equivalents (page 196)

$1\frac{1}{4}$	$\frac{23}{100}$	$\frac{4}{5}$	$\frac{1}{4}$	$\frac{3}{5}$
2	$\frac{3}{10}$	$\frac{3}{20}$	$2\frac{1}{2}$	$\frac{3}{10}$
$\frac{7}{10}$	$\frac{1}{20}$	$\frac{3}{4}$	$\frac{1}{5}$	$1\frac{1}{2}$
1	$\frac{1}{4}$	$\frac{1}{10}$	$2\frac{1}{4}$	$\frac{2}{5}$
$\frac{9}{20}$	$\frac{3}{5}$	$\frac{3}{500}$	$\frac{3}{25}$	$\frac{1}{2}$
$\frac{11}{20}$	$\frac{1}{25}$	$\frac{9}{10}$	$\frac{11}{20}$	$\frac{1}{2}$

Test 4 Fraction Equivalents (page 197)

$\frac{1}{4}$	$\frac{9}{100}$	$\frac{1}{2}$	$\frac{3}{20}$	$\frac{17}{20}$
$2\frac{1}{4}$	4	$1\frac{1}{4}$	$\frac{11}{100}$	$\frac{4}{5}$
$\frac{17}{100}$	$\frac{2}{25}$	$\frac{9}{20}$	$\frac{1}{50}$	$\frac{19}{100}$
$1\frac{1}{2}$	$\frac{1}{10}$	$\frac{3}{5}$	$\frac{67}{100}$	$\frac{3}{100}$
$\frac{7}{20}$	$\frac{1}{2}$	$\frac{13}{20}$	$\frac{19}{20}$	$\frac{9}{50}$
$\frac{17}{20}$	$\frac{21}{100}$	$\frac{3}{4}$	2	$\frac{7}{10}$

Test 5 Fraction Equivalents (page 198)

$\frac{2}{5}$	$2\frac{1}{2}$	$\frac{1}{2}$	$\frac{1}{4}$	$\frac{3}{5}$
$1\frac{1}{4}$	$\frac{13}{50}$	$\frac{17}{20}$	$\frac{11}{20}$	$\frac{2}{5}$
8	$\frac{3}{5}$	$\frac{3}{20}$	$6\frac{1}{2}$	$\frac{1}{5}$
$\frac{3}{10}$	$\frac{1}{20}$	$\frac{3}{4}$	$\frac{3}{4}$	$3\frac{1}{2}$
3	$\frac{7}{20}$	$\frac{3}{10}$	$2\frac{1}{4}$	$\frac{1}{10}$
$\frac{3}{20}$	$\frac{7}{10}$	$\frac{1}{200}$	$\frac{19}{100}$	$\frac{9}{10}$
$\frac{13}{20}$	$\frac{3}{100}$	$\frac{4}{5}$	$\frac{11}{20}$	$\frac{1}{4}$
$2\frac{3}{4}$	$\frac{7}{20}$	$\frac{1}{10}$	$\frac{9}{10}$	$\frac{1}{100}$

Test 6 Fraction Equivalents (page 199)

$\frac{1}{250}$	$\frac{3}{10}$	$1\frac{3}{20}$	$1\frac{1}{2}$	$2\frac{1}{2}$
$\frac{1}{20}$	$\frac{9}{100}$	$\frac{1}{2}$	$\frac{3}{20}$	$\frac{17}{20}$
$2\frac{1}{4}$	$\frac{21}{100}$	$\frac{29}{100}$	2	$\frac{47}{100}$
6	$1\frac{1}{4}$	$\frac{11}{100}$	$\frac{1}{20}$	$\frac{9}{50}$
$\frac{17}{100}$	$\frac{2}{25}$	$\frac{9}{20}$	$\frac{1}{25}$	$\frac{19}{100}$
$1\frac{1}{2}$	$\frac{1}{10}$	$\frac{3}{5}$	$\frac{13}{20}$	$\frac{7}{100}$
$\frac{7}{20}$	$\frac{1}{2}$	$\frac{83}{100}$	$\frac{3}{4}$	$\frac{1}{4}$
$\frac{17}{20}$	$\frac{33}{100}$	$\frac{3}{25}$	$\frac{3}{10}$	$\frac{9}{10}$

Test 1 Decimal Equivalents (page 200)

0.5	0.23	0.8	0.25
0.19	0.08	0.5	0.5
0.25	0.75	0.4	0.3
0.7	1.8	0.85	0.6
0.75	0.45	0.25	0.02

Test 2 Decimal Equivalents (page 201)

0.3	0.03	0.1	0.6
0.5	2	0.9	0.15
1.75	1.5	0.05	0.4
0.55	2.75	0.26	0.05
0.55	0.2	0.18	0.8

Test 3 Decimal Equivalents (page 202)

0.01	0.08	0.45	0.02	0.1
0.85	0.3	0.75	1.5	0.65
8	0.2	0.15	6.5	0.2
1.5	0.7	0.6	0.65	0.75
0.35	0.5	0.83	0.6	0.25
0.7	0.55	0.95	0.4	1.5

Test 4 Decimal Equivalents (page 203)

1	0.25	0.1	0.001	0.4
0.63	0.2	0.06	0.65	0.75
0.35	0.33	0.12	0.33	0.09
0.14	0.07	0.5	0.15	0.85
0.6	0.05	0.75	0.7	5.5
0.17	0.08	0.45	0.04	0.19

Test 5 Decimal Equivalents (page 204)

0.25	0.25	0.25	0.55	1.5
0.99	0.5	0.66	0.5	0.33
0.1	0.6	0.003	0.17	0.5
0.65	0.95	0.18	0.2	0.35
2.75	0.85	0.1	0.9	0.01
7	0.45	0.3	0.4	0.1
2.25	0.21	0.75	2	0.43
6	0.04	0.11	0.08	0.7

Test 6 Decimal Equivalents (page 205)

0.05	0.18	0.2	0.22	0.25
0.9	0.55	0.5	0.55	0.04
0.85	0.43	0.75	1	0.6
0.45	0.19	0.44	0.2	0.99
1.5	0.7	0.05	0.19	0.09
0.65	0.25	0.8	0.55	0.2
0.68	0.12	0.333	0.66	0.7
0.75	2.75	0.1	0.65	0.04

Answer Key *(cont.)*

Unit 7: Fraction, Decimal, and Percent Equivalents *(cont.)*

Test 1 Percent Equivalents (page 206)

40%	50%	5%	6%
20%	75%	36%	20%
50%	90%	20%	45%
11%	3%	175%	25%
40%	55%	6%	3%

Test 2 Percent Equivalents (page 207)

2%	60%	13%	125%
4%	80%	30%	250%
90%	275%	225%	2%
75%	18%	80%	450%
1%	45%	0.4%	40%

Test 3 Percent Equivalents (page 208)

150%	70%	13%	350%	80%
175%	73%	18%	90%	10%
10%	60%	33%	1%	30%
25%	40%	22%	15%	275%
25%	150%	4%	225%	19%
33%	70%	50%	175%	38%

Test 4 Percent Equivalents (page 209)

50%	50%	30%	133%	40%
90%	25%	77%	4%	18%
75%	16%	5%	95%	20%
4%	10%	225%	85%	175%
20%	6%	75%	25%	75%
5%	90%	15%	28%	20%

Test 5 Percent Equivalents (page 210)

180%	13%	40%	17%	150%
0.9%	60%	40%	65%	12%
260%	250%	160%	33%	100%
0.3%	100%	21%	50%	60%
70%	90%	275%	225%	2%
45%	20%	370%	55%	55%
75%	60%	3%	4%	30%
95%	50%	89%	20%	23%

Test 6 Percent Equivalents (page 211)

10%	90%	133%	35%	225%
7%	9%	40%	15%	75%
29%	260%	5%	13%	47%
4%	25%	10%	2%	25%
75%	70%	19%	300%	44%
225%	29%	50%	55%	1%
17%	2%	250%	25%	50%
80%	42%	75%	20%	6%